FII

IN ANGER AND
BITTERNESS

NICK DONNELLY

All booklets are published
thanks to the generosity of the supporters
of the Catholic Truth Society

CTS

Dedicated to my wife,
for teaching me the ways of the heart.

The biblical references are taken from the *Revised Standard Version* and the *New Jerusalem Bible*.

Image Credits
Page 4 © Brian Lasenby/Shutterstock.com
Page 25 © Eakachai Leesin/Shutterstock.com
Page 44 © Sidney de Almeida/Shutterstock.com

All rights reserved. First published 2018 by The Incorporated Catholic Truth Society, 40-46 Harleyford Road, London SE11 5AY. Tel: 020 7640 0042 Fax: 020 7640 0040 www.ctsbooks.org Copyright © 2018 The Incorporated Catholic Truth Society.

ISBN 978 1 78469 573 6

Contents

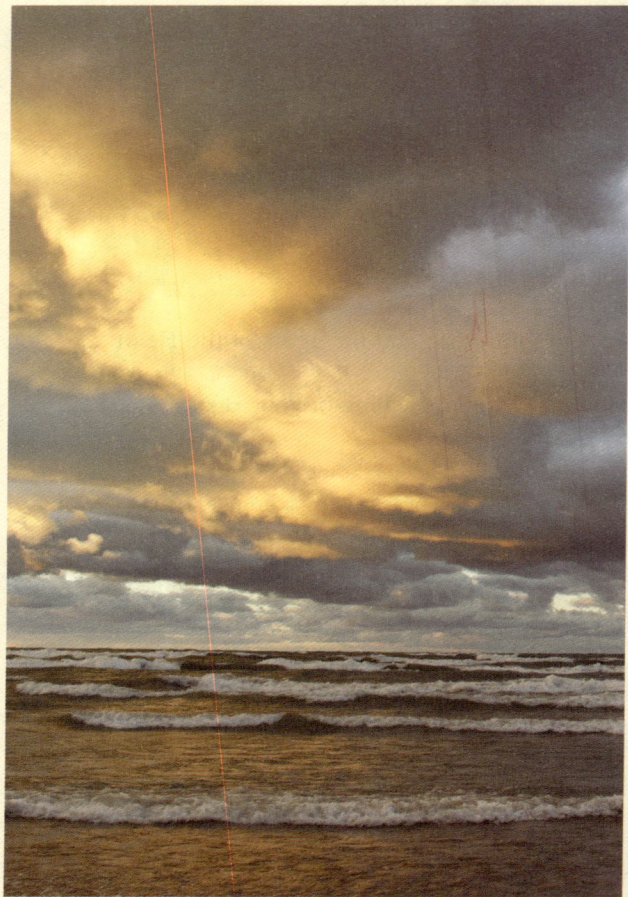

Not All Tears are Evil

There is a passage in J R R Tolkien's *Lord of the Rings*, the meaning of which I have pondered over for the past forty-seven years since I first read it as a twelve year old boy. It occurs at the very end of the final volume, *The Return of the King*, when close friends face the shock of realising that they must say farewell to each other for the final time. Tolkien writes:

> Well, here at last, dear friends, on the shores of the Sea comes the end of our fellowship in Middle-earth. Go in peace! I will not say: do not weep; for not all tears are an evil.[1]

As a school boy I just didn't understand the phrase, "for not all tears are an evil", because then the only tears I knew were those caused by the illnesses, and the scrapes and blows of childhood. The rare times I cried, I felt better for it. How could tears be evil?

However, as an adult, experience has taught me the meaning of Tolkien's enigmatic phrase "for not all tears are an evil". Of course, I still experience 'good tears': the gentle tears of mourning for loved ones whose deaths have been peaceful and a timely release; tears of joy at the beauty of creation and God's grace; tears of laughter with friends, and, sometimes tears of healing contrition.

But I have also come to know tears that are evil: tears caused by personal betrayal; crushing disappointment, and, overwhelming grief. Tears that can be the outward sign of passions that can so easily turn to evil: to seething anger; burning resentment; cold hatred, and, dark fantasies of revenge and destruction. Bitter tears that become the gateway to grave sins.

When sin crouches at the door

Who hasn't felt sin crouching at their door as a consequence of rage, envy, or desire for vengeance, no matter how fleeting these feelings?

> So Cain was very angry, and his countenance fell. The Lord said to Cain, "Why are you angry, and why has your countenance fallen? If you do well, will you not be accepted? And if you do not do well, sin is crouching at the door; its desire is for you, but you must master it." (*Gn* 4:5-7)

If we focus for the moment on betrayal, Jordan Peterson, the Canadian psychologist, explains that betrayal, especially by those closest to us, is the worst thing to happen to a person. This is because consequent emotions of bitterness, rage, resentment, vengeance, hatred, even murderous hatred, can make life for ourselves and those around us hell on earth:

> You plunge into that underworld space, and that's also where you begin to nurse feelings of resentment and aggrievement and murder and homicide, and even worse. If people are betrayed enough, they become obsessed with the futility of being itself, and they go to places where perhaps no one would ever want to go if they were in their right mind. And they begin to nurse fantasies of the ultimate revenge, and that's a horrible place to be. And that's hell. That's why hell has always been a suburb of the underworld, because if you get plunged into a situation that you don't understand, and things are not good for you anymore, it's only one step from being completely confused, to being completely outraged and resentful, and then it's only one step from there to really looking for revenge. And that can take you places – well, that merely to imagine properly can be traumatic.[2]

Our choice: benign anger or malignant anger?

The psychologist Erich Fromm (1900-1980) makes the distinction between "benign aggression" and "malignant aggression", between the "passion of anger" and "destructively aggressive acts". Sometimes feeling angry – benign anger – is the appropriate response to an evil or a threat, because anger instantly tells us the truth of the situation and gives us the energy to react to it. Brooding anger – malignant anger – is different for a number of reasons: we obsessively dwell on the injustice; fantasise about revenge and retaliation, and, take pleasure in our sustained emotion of anger and at the prospect of hurting others.

Deliberate and intentional betrayal at the hands of a husband or wife, brother or sister, or close friend can be rightly perceived as a life-threatening attack that causes physical, psychological and spiritual harm. Anger at the injustice and harm of betrayal is a natural and justifiable response of self-protection. The Church recognises the importance and value of passions, such as anger in the face of such evil:

> The passions are natural components of the human psyche; they form the passageway and ensure the connection between the life of the senses and the life of the mind. Our Lord called man's heart the source from which the passions spring (*Mk* 7:21)... The apprehension of evil causes hatred, aversion, and fear of the impending evil; this movement ends in sadness at some present evil, or in the anger that resists it.[3]

Having said this, everyone is faced with a choice when caught up in the passion of anger to either 'master' it and thereby benefit from its insight and energy, or intentionally allow it free rein to become malignant aggression. In every occasion of passion there is a moment of self-knowledge and choice:

> Passions are morally good when they contribute to a good action, evil in the opposite case. The upright will orders the movements of the senses it appropriates to the good and to beatitude; an evil will succumbs to disordered passions and exacerbates them. Emotions and feelings can be taken up into the virtues or perverted by the vices.[4]

Alastair Campbell, an expert in pastoral care, concludes that faced with a culture that fosters and incites destructiveness, Christians must even more embrace the challenge of severing the "lethal link" between our own feelings of anger and the impulse to destructive aggression.[5]

St Paul, in his Letter to the Ephesians, advises that the way to break the lethal link between anger and destructiveness is to make it a personal priority to speak truthfully about our anger as soon as possible, and thereby stop anger becoming hate:

> "Therefore, putting away falsehood, let everyone speak the truth with his neighbour, for we are members

one of another. Be angry but do not sin; do not let the sun go down on your anger, and give no opportunity to the devil." (*Ep* 4:25-27)

Don't give the devil his opportunity

A daily diet of bitterness, resentment and fantasies of revenge takes us into the sphere of influence of the devil. I learnt this personally following a series of upsetting events recently that occurred one after the other over a matter of months. My hard won career was derailed, my income reduced to almost nothing, and significant friendships broken. As a consequence, every morning I woke up to an electric shock of anger and a succession of revenge scenarios playing out in my mind as if projected onto a screen. I had to shake myself to break free from these obsessive thoughts and get on with my day.

I half-heartedly prayed for the grace of forgiveness, but, to be honest, I took pleasure in my heightened emotion of anger and my dreams of revenge. The truth of the matter is, we easily delight in evil, particularly when we feel justified as the wounded party. This is one of the clearest signs of the influence of concupiscence on our behaviour. "Concupiscence" means "intense desire", and describes the fact that, at times, we experience an intense desire to commit sin. Due to original sin "human nature, without being totally corrupted, is wounded in its natural powers. It is subject to ignorance, to suffering, and to the dominion of death and is inclined towards sin."[6] We all have an inclination to evil, an attraction to sin, and, in my case, I delighted in imagining taking revenge on my 'enemies' who had hurt me.

I did not follow the advice of St Paul and instead I let many suns go down on my anger. As a consequence I placed myself in the way of being harmed by the devil. St Ignatius of Loyola observes in *The Spiritual Exercises* that the devil is like a general of a demonic army, who inspects the "fortifications and defences of a fortress" and "attacks it at its weakest point":

"…the enemy of our human nature makes his rounds to inspect our virtues, theological, cardinal and moral, and where he finds us weakest and in greatest need as regard our eternal salvation, there he attacks and tries to take us."[7]

The devil and the demons have had millions of years to study human beings, giving them the knowledge of how to work on the weaknesses of each one of us. Fr José Fortea, the exorcist, writes that "a demon can be at our side for a very long time, analysing us and coming to know our particular weaknesses. He will seek to tempt us at our weakest point".[8]

Since the deaths of my two children, Gabriel and Ariel, my weak point is a temptation to suicide. I have taken a deep wound to my spirit with the deaths of my son and daughter. My own understanding is that death, especially the tragic deaths of children, puts the survivors into the sphere of influence of the devil. Scripture tells us, "God did not make death, and he does not delight in the death of the living… It was through the devil's envy that death entered the world" (*Ws* 1:13; 2:24) and the devil "has the power of death" (*Heb* 2:14).

Following the series of personal blows I gradually experienced again, with growing intensity, the temptation to commit suicide. I didn't want to have this thought, and when I noticed it I pushed it away, but the temptation came back the next day. I told my priest that I was experiencing this temptation to suicide. He asked me did I want to act on this thought, and I emphatically responded that I did not, that it felt like something alien that was intruding into my life. He concluded that I was suffering demonic obsession, a form of demonic attack, described as being besieged by the devil through emotional pressure, pressing in on a person.[9] There and then he administered the sacrament of the sick, and I haven't been bothered by this temptation since that moment.

Looking back, I can see that the demon found an opening into my life as a result of my sinful response to betrayal. My own toxic mix of resentment, rage and hate lowered my defences and the demon saw his opportunity and worked away at a deep wound. I thank God for the healing I received through the sacrament of the sick at the hands of a priest who took seriously the reality of demonic attacks.

Following my healing I reached out to those who had hurt me, and as a consequence my relationship with some of them has been somewhat repaired, and is now open to the possibility of deeper healing.

Jesus wants to heal your broken heart

In light of my own experience of deep healing through the sacrament of the sick, I know for certain that Jesus wants to heal all broken hearts. He came down from heaven to heal man's heart, and through his incarnation he knows with his human heart the evils that break ours. Jesus wept over the evil in our hearts:

"O Jerusalem, Jerusalem, killing the prophets and stoning those who are sent to you! How often would I have gathered your children together as a hen gathers her brood under her wings, and you would not!" (*Mt* 23:37; cf. *Lk* 19:41-44)

Jesus cries tears of compassion looking down on Jerusalem, not tears that presage bitterness, rage, and plans for revenge. The Catholic philosopher, Peter Kreeft, describes Jesus as the "tears of God".[10]

Our Lord embodies the Most Holy Trinity's tears of compassion for each one of us, despite our rejection and betrayal of God.

Neal Lozano, a Christian healer and teacher, believes it's very important that we realise that God loves us so much that our betrayal breaks his heart. God is not aloof and indifferent to our sufferings. Those who have experienced the agony of losing a child, or the anguish of the deep betrayal of someone you thought loved you leaving you, know something of the Father's heartbreak:

> Many of you have experienced deep pain over your children and know how this feels. Some have lost a child to a premature death, cancer, addiction, isolation, depression or suicide. In these experiences, you have felt a portion of the excruciating pain and agony that afflicts the Father's heart. In Mel Gibson's film *The Passion of the Christ*, the Father's heart was portrayed in the moment of Jesus' death; the camera pans out to a view from the skies, and a teardrop forms and falls to the ground. When I saw this, I wondered, when did the tears of the Father fall? Did the Father weep only for Jesus, or did he also weep for Adam and Eve at the moment they fell into sin? …Likewise, did he weep only for Adam or for every one of us who were still in Adam?[11]

As I discovered, he weeps for us all. The sacraments are the physical expression of God's compassion for each one of us – we are healed by the tears of God.

Not all tears are evil: prayer reflections

Not all tears are evil – but some can be. Why do I weep?

- Dwelling on resentment or despair, choosing malignant anger, can allow the devil an opening he will exploit. What do I do with my anger?

- God longs to heal us and wipe away every tear. Am I prepared to let Christ heal me?

Lord, remove the bitterness of my anger, the despair of my anger. When I am weak and in torment, purify me and strengthen me to resist evil and its pain and influence. Hold me in your heart and wipe away my tears until that day when there will be no more weeping and you will be all in all. Amen.

Learning the Ways of your Heart

The heart of man – my heart and your heart – is the focus of all the Most Holy Trinity's words and deeds that drive the whole sweeping history of salvation. The Father's outpouring of revelation and grace, culminating in the incarnation of his Son, and bestowal of sacraments through the Holy Spirit, has one purpose – to change our hearts, made hard by sin, into hearts of flesh capable of genuine love, capable of receiving his Spirit.

Why is the heart, and not the mind, the focus of God's activity? Though secular materialists would have us believe that the brain produces the mind and sense of self, God's word tells us that the heart is the innermost centre of the person. There are over one thousand references to the heart in Sacred Scripture describing the interior life of man, our ideas, feelings and sense of self.

Common phrases from modern everyday language
show that people still place the heart as the centre of
the self. People can be described as 'hard-hearted' or
'soft-hearted', 'good-hearted' or 'bad-hearted', 'kind-
hearted' or 'mean-hearted', 'warm-hearted' or 'cold-
hearted'. There are many heart words to describe
love – 'lose one's heart', 'heart-ache', 'touched my
heart', 'stole my heart'. Heart language is also used
to describe the virtues and vices of a person: 'brave-
heart', 'stout-heart', 'big heart', 'heart of gold', 'black
heart', 'cruel heart'. The most personal conversations
between people are referred to as speaking 'heart to
heart', and 'opening up one's heart'.

The *Catechism of the Catholic Church* summarises
this perennial understanding of the role of the heart in
our interior life:

The heart is the dwelling-place where I am, where
I live; according to the Semitic or biblical expression,
the heart is the place "to which I withdraw." The
heart is our hidden centre, beyond the grasp of
our reason and of others; only the Spirit of God
can fathom the human heart and know it fully.
The heart is the place of decision, deeper than our
psychic drives. It is the place of truth, where we
choose life or death. It is the place of encounter,
because as image of God we live in relation: it is
the place of covenant.[12]

Man is a unity of body and soul

In coming to understand the heart as the dwelling-place where 'I am', we remember that man is a unity of body and soul.[13] This means that it is often not possible to distinguish between the physical heart and the spiritual heart, because both interact and influence each other. Anyone who has felt how the joyful ache of love makes his or her physical heart race knows this, or anyone who has experienced how fear for the safety of a loved one contracts the heart in agony, knows that the physical heart and the spiritual heart are inextricably linked.

It is true that you can die of a broken heart. Doctors have identified an illness called 'broken heart syndrome' otherwise known as Takotsubo Cardiomyopathy, caused by intense grief or emotional shock that so damages the heart that it changes its shape. Approximately three thousand people suffer from it in the UK, mostly women, 70% of whom developed it following the sudden death of a loved one. Between 3% and 17% of sufferers die within five years of diagnosis, but for most it is temporary and reversible.

From this we see that medical science is uncovering the connection between the physical heart and the spiritual heart. We are symbolic beings expressing our interior life of emotions and thoughts not only with words, but also through our bodies. Our faces are in almost constant movement expressing and emphasising emotions and thoughts. Many of us use our hands as an impromptu sign language of feelings and ideas.

In our own experience of the interior life many experience the physical heart as the symbol of the inner self, a coincidence of our physical heart with our spiritual heart: "The heart, as well as being a physical organ in our chest, represents symbolically the focal point of our personhood as created in the image and likeness of God".[14]

The eminent psychiatrist Carl Jung gives an account of his conversation with a chief of the Taos Pueblos Native Americans, Ochwiay Biano, which I have found very useful in understanding the heart and my sense of self:

"See," Ochwiay Biano said "how cruel the whites look. Their lips are thin, their noses sharp, their faces furrowed and distorted by folds. Their eyes have a staring expression; they are always seeking something. What are they seeking? The whites always want something. They are always uneasy and restless. We do not know what they want. We do not understand them. We think that they are all mad." I asked him why he thought the whites were all mad. "They say they think with their heads," he replied. "Why of course. What do you think with," I asked him in surprise. "We think here," he said, indicating his heart.[15]

When I was newly married I asked my wife a question, thinking of this passage in Jung's autobiography. I asked her, where did she experience her sense of self, where did she sense the centre of her self-awareness and self-reflection? I had not told her about Jung's conversation with Ochwiay Biano. With certainty, she pointed to her heart. I was amazed. Unlike my wife, I definitely experienced my sense of self in my head. I was fascinated to discover this difference between us, and wondered if Ochwiay Biano was right! I am restless, uneasy, always seeking, while my wife is more peaceful, measured and centred. Chief Ochwiay Biano and my wife shared the Bible's understanding of the human person. And as the decades have passed, I have experienced, through prayer, my sense of self gradually shifting from my head to my heart, so if you were to ask me where did I locate myself I, too, would now point to my heart.

The thoughts of the heart

According to the Hebrew understanding of man in the Bible the heart is the organ of feelings, thoughts and decisions. God has given man a heart to think with (*Si* 17:6). The heart is the source of consciousness, intelligence and personality, and as such is the centre of man's being, "the place where he enters into dialogue with himself, accepts his responsibilities and opens himself or closes himself to God".[16] Walter Eichrodt, the Old Testament scholar, explains that in Hebrew the word for heart was a comprehensive term for personal character, personality, and the inner life, with an emphasis on its role in decision making and the life of the intellect.[17]

Since the times of the Old Testament, modern science has shown us the role of the brain in thinking, memories, decision-making and the life of the mind. However, we can learn from the Hebrew understanding of man the role of the heart as a source of knowledge and perception of the truth of things. The passions are both a precious source of knowledge and a spur to decision-making, especially when aligned with God's commandments and lived in the Spirit of Christ. The intense love we feel for our spouses, children and family is a knowledge deeper than reason and the intellect. The anger that we feel at injustice, on seeing the suffering of the innocent due to war or disease or neglect or hatred is also an experience of this deep knowledge of the heart. The Bible's many descriptions and explanations of the ways of the heart can help us tune into this knowledge. We make life-changing decisions informed by these reasons of the heart – vocations are chosen, campaigns for justice are fought, lives are sacrificed in the service of others.

The Hebrews understood that though our heart is hidden within our interior life, our outward behaviour can reveal what is in our heart:

A man's heart changes his countenance,
either for good or for evil.
The mark of a happy heart is a cheerful face,
but to devise proverbs requires painful thinking.
(*Si* 13:25-26)

The Bible really disapproves of people whose face says one thing, while their heart is feeling or thinking the exact opposite:

Like the glaze covering an earthen vessel
are smooth lips with an evil heart.
He who hates, dissembles with his lips
and harbours deceit in his heart;
when he speaks graciously, believe him not,
for there are seven abominations in his heart;
though his hatred be covered with guile,
his wickedness will be exposed in the assembly.
(*Pr* 26:23-26)

God searches our hearts

Though we can hide the true intentions and desires of our hearts from others, we can't hide the secrets of our hearts from God. The Old Testament understood God as the almighty creator of the universe, and the mighty judge and arbiter of nation, but he is also concerned with the heart of each person.

The Hebrews were very aware that God searches and knows the heart of every person he has created, "for the Lord sees not as man sees; man looks on the outward appearance, but the Lord looks on the heart" (*1 S* 16:7); "I the LORD search the heart and test the mind, to give every man according to his ways, according to the fruit of his deeds" (*Jr* 17:10).

The heart is also the place of encounter between man and God, because the spiritual centre of man – the seat of love, intellect and will – is most like God, who is pure spirit. In this vast universe of galaxies, solar systems, planets, oceans and continents teeming with a multitude of life your heart is not accidental or marginal, but is the place where you can plunge into the depths of reality:

> [Man] plunges into the depths of reality whenever he enters into his own heart; God, who probes the heart, awaits him there; there he discerns his proper destiny beneath the eyes of God. Thus, when he recognises in himself a spiritual and immortal soul, he is not being mocked by a fantasy born only of physical or social influences, but is rather laying hold of the proper truth of the matter.[18]

God takes a particular interest in the heart of each one of us:

> Indeed you love truth in the heart;
> then in the secret of my heart teach me wisdom.
> O purify me, then I shall be clean;
> O wash me, I shall be whiter than snow.
> (*Ps* 51:6-7)

God has written his law in our hearts

Our heart is not born as a *tabula rasa* – a blank slate – on which we can create anything we desire. The heart of each one of us is so precious to God that he has written his law there to protect us from harming ourselves, from damaging our heart:

> Deep within his conscience man discovers a law which he has not laid upon himself but which he must obey. Its voice, ever calling him to love and to do what is good and to avoid evil, sounds in his heart at the right moment… For man has in his heart a law inscribed by God…. His conscience is man's most secret core and his sanctuary. There he is alone with God whose voice echoes in his depths.[19]

The law of God, written within our heart, is the voice of conscience, which prompts and disturbs us unbidden. A good conscience, informed by divine revelation and sanctified by the sacraments, raises the alarm when we are tempted to sin, and painfully stings us with

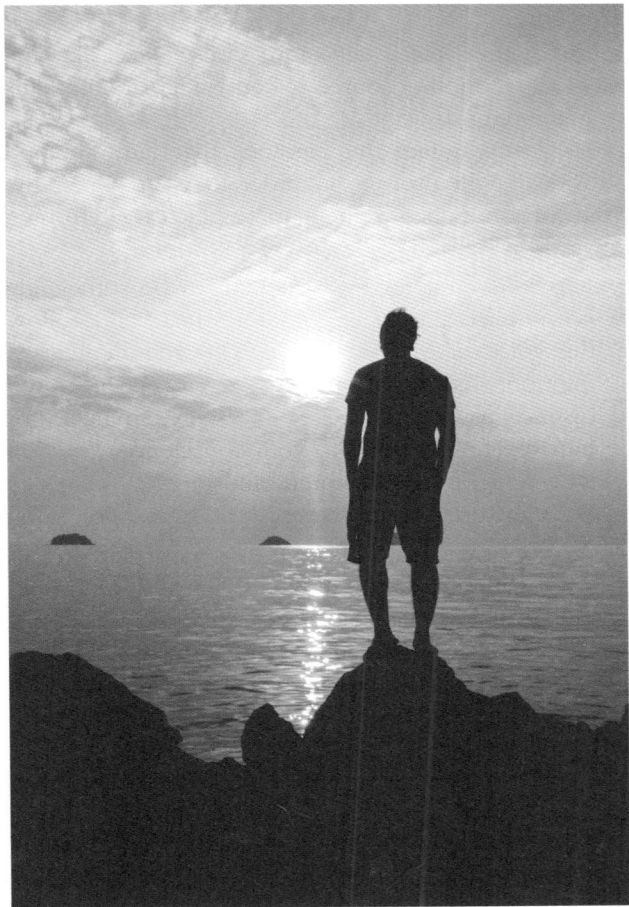

remorse after sinful acts. Our conscience, like the passions, is another source of knowledge and impetus to make right decisions.

However, unlike the passions that flare up and subside by themselves, in order to clearly hear the voice of conscience we need to be practised in turning inwards in self-reflection and recollection:

> It is important for every person to be sufficiently present to himself in order to hear and follow the voice of his conscience. This requirement of interiority is all the more necessary as life often distracts us from any reflection, self-examination or introspection: "Return to your conscience, question it… Turn inward, brethren, and in everything you do, see God as your witness." (St Augustine)[20]

A sinful desire or an addiction to a particular sin can overwhelm the quiet voice of conscience if we haven't protected it by cultivating the practice of being 'present to ourselves' through prayer and the self-awareness and self-examination that goes with proper recourse to the sacrament of confession.

Hardening of the heart

We can do serious damage to our hearts if we get into the habit of ignoring or silencing our conscience. This leads to a grave moral and spiritual condition that the Bible calls a "hard heart" (*Ps* 95) or a "cauterised heart" (*1 Tm* 4:2). A spiritual law comes into play if we choose to harden our hearts, like a biological law comes into play if we lead unhealthy lives.

In the Old Testament, "hardening of the heart" refers to the judgement of God on those who intentionally reject him by the choices they make in life. If you choose "faithlessness and voluntary blindness", God will allow you to fully experience the consequences.[21] In the Book of Isaiah, the Lord addresses his prophet, and sends him with this judgement on faithless Israel:

Go, and say to this people,
"Listen and listen, but never understand!
Look and look, but never perceive!"
Make this people's heart coarse,
make their ears dull, shut their eyes tight,
or they will use their eyes to see,
use their ears to hear,
use their hearts to understand,
and change their ways and be healed.
(*Is* 6:9-10)

I read this as God sending the prophet Isaiah to shock his people out of their hard-heartedness and blindness, by spelling out the consequences of their sinful actions. It has to be read through the lens of the incarnation of the Son of God, "But God shows his love for us in that while we were yet sinners Christ died for us" (*Rm* 5:8). I think this passage points out that if we did listen, if we did use our eyes to see, our ears to hear and our hearts to understand, we would change and be healed. Salvation History shows us that God wants our healing and conversion, never our punishment and destruction (*Ezk* 18:23).

St Paul warns that those who obstinately reject God and the Faith "cauterise" their consciences (*1 Tm* 4:2). During the time of St Paul it was common to punish evildoers by branding them with a mark to identify them as criminals. Branding makes the skin hard and insensitive with scar tissue. The point St Paul is making is that we deform our consciences when we obstinately reject God and the Faith by our way of life, making one of the innermost parts of our soul disordered and insensitive. The *Catechism of the Catholic Church* lists "enslavement to one's passions" as one of the causes of conscience being blinded.[22]

We can see this "hardening of the heart" at work among individuals who have angrily rejected God in reaction to some deep hurt, or betrayal in their past, by members of their family. When God or the Church are mentioned their faces became pinched and hard and their words mocking and aggressive. And we can feel this "hardening of the heart" in ourselves when we do not want to listen to 'reasons' or 'justifications' or forgive.

Learning the ways of your heart: prayer reflections

- The heart is the place where I come to know myself. Who am I in my heart?

- God searches our hearts where he has written his law. Do I dwell in my heart?

- Man can 'harden his heart'. How has my heart hardened?

Lord, in the spirit of my heart teach me wisdom.
Let me know in the truth of my conscience,
the reality of me as you know me. Bring my heart
ever closer to yours. Amen.

Let Jesus Heal your Heart

After centuries of rebellion and betrayal against God the prophets concluded that man was so trapped in habitual sin that nothing could be done, that the damage to the heart of every person was too great. If you're honest, you also know deep down that there is something wrong with your heart and the hearts of every human being:

> But this people has a stubborn and rebellious heart; they have turned aside and gone away. They do not say in their hearts, "Let us fear the Lord our God"…they did not obey or incline their ear, but walked in their own counsels and the stubbornness of their evil hearts, and went backwards and not forwards. (*Jr* 5:23; 7:24)

We know that we are divided within ourselves, capable of great acts of goodness and compassion and low acts of hatred and cruelty. No matter how hard we try we cannot stop the war within ourselves against

God's law. We suffer in the ceaseless fight between obedience and rebellion, faithfulness and infidelity, light and dark.

The prophets concluded that man's heart was so hardened and damaged by sin that nothing could be done by man. Nothing could be done by man alone. But the prophets also promised that sometime in the future God would do something marvellous, he would turn hearts of stone into hearts of flesh:

> I will sprinkle clean water upon you, and you shall be clean from all your uncleannesses, and from all your idols I will cleanse you. A new heart I will give you, and a new spirit I will put within you; and I will take out of your flesh the heart of stone and give you a heart of flesh. And I will put my spirit within you, and cause you to walk in my statutes and be careful to observe my ordinances. (*Ezk* 36:25-27)

The incarnation of the Son of God is this marvellous work promised by the prophets, when God assumed human nature, and assumed into the life of the Most Holy Trinity a human heart with its conscience and passions. By assuming a human nature Jesus' heart is mysteriously united to the heart of every person:

> For by his incarnation the Son of God has united himself in some fashion with every man. He worked

with human hands, he thought with a human mind, acted by human choice and loved with a human heart. Born of the Virgin Mary, he has truly been made one of us, like us in all things except sin.[23]

Jesus knows the human heart

Jesus knows the human heart as a man, with his experience of the interior life, and, as the Son of God, with divine knowledge. As the Son of God, Jesus could search and judge the hearts of individuals, and this ability was seen as a sign of his divinity:

"And immediately Jesus, perceiving in his spirit that they thus questioned within themselves, said to them, 'Why do you question thus in your hearts?'" (*Mk* 2:8).

"Jesus did not trust himself to them, because he knew all men and needed no one to bear witness of man; for he himself knew what was in man" (*Jn* 2:23-25).

Our Lord, as a man, also knew the heart's capacity for evil, because even though he was without sin he was subject to every temptation that we endure (*Heb* 4:15). Jesus observed:

"For out of the heart come evil thoughts, murder, adultery, fornication, theft, false witness, slander. These are what defile a man" (*Mt* 15:19).

Jesus knows very well that evil thoughts obsess our minds before they become actions. Even if they are never acted out, such evil thoughts harm our hearts. Our Lord wants us to take such thoughts and fantasies with the utmost seriousness, as, for example, his condemnation of lust: "But I say to you that everyone who looks at a woman lustfully has already committed adultery with her in his heart" (*Mt* 5:28). The same warning applies to anger (*Mt* 5:22).

Jesus tests the hardness of our hearts

There is a saying of Our Lord's that I find difficult because it seems beyond my ability. It is found in the Parable of the Unforgiving Servant (*Mt* 18:23-35). Jesus tells the story of a servant who is forgiven a huge debt by his master, but this servant refuses to forgive the minuscule debt of a fellow servant. The parable concludes:

> Then his lord summoned him and said to him, "You wicked servant! I forgave you all that debt because you besought me; and should not you have had mercy on your fellow servant, as I had mercy on you?" And in anger his lord delivered him to the jailers, till he should pay all his debt. So also my heavenly Father will do to every one of you, if you do not forgive your brother from your heart. (*Mt* 18:32-35)

The wicked servant is too hard-hearted to forgive his fellow servant, even though he has received such abundant forgiveness from his master. The saying of Jesus that I find so difficult is his injunction that we forgive others from our hearts. This parable tests the degree to which we have allowed Jesus to turn our hearts of stone into hearts of flesh. It reveals the hardness of our hearts. My heart contains an ever growing list of people who have hurt me throughout my life, towards whom I feel bitterness and resentment. Even though I have forgiven them on an intellectual level, because that is what Christians are supposed to do, I know that I have not really forgiven them from my heart.

The fact is, if our relationship with Jesus does not radically change our relationship with others, what's the point of calling ourselves Christian? Jesus has told us that we will only be forgiven if we forgive others like our Father in heaven has forgiven us (*Mt* 6:15). If our Christian life is not about becoming, through his grace and his teaching, more and more like Jesus in our forgiveness of others then we are Christian in name only.

The Parable of the Unforgiving Servant is a mirror that shows us the true condition of our heart and the degree to which we have allowed Jesus to transform our hard hearts into his heart. It leaves me longing to realise in my own life the truth of St Paul's words:

"Put off your old nature which belongs to your former manner of life and is corrupt through deceitful lusts, and be renewed in the spirit of your minds, and put on the new nature, created after the likeness of God in true righteousness and holiness" (*Ep* 4:22-24).

Jesus calls us to be extraordinary

One of the most striking aspects of Jesus' teaching about forgiveness is his exhortation that we must love our enemies. This is Jesus' ultimate test of whether our relationship with him has changed our relationship with others. It is the hardest thing Our Lord asks us to do:

"To the natural man, the very notion of loving his enemies is an intolerable offence, and quite beyond his capacity: it cuts right across his ideas of good and evil".[24]

Living in countries free from conflict or overt persecution, we do not routinely use the word 'enemy' and it can be difficult to put a 'face' to an enemy. Having said this, the real enemies in life, more often than not, can be friends, family, and, loved ones. The worst enemies in life can be husband, wife, father, mother, brother, sister, son, daughter, childhood friend, or intimate confidant. There can be a million different reasons why family and friends fall out to the point of becoming enemies and the impact on everyone involved can be devastating. Confronted with such enemies, our hearts can become the hardest, the most unforgiving, because it can be so unjust and hurts so much.

Other people can become enemies for different reasons, such as bullying, rivalry at work, opposing beliefs, or personal dislike and this too can have a devastating impact on our lives. We can make enemies at school, work, and even church, and we can become the enemy of others for the same reasons.

The ordinary way of the human heart when faced with enemies is the spiralling descent into anger, bitterness, resentment, hatred, rage, vengeance and, even, violence, sometimes homicidal violence. Instead, Jesus calls us to take the extraordinary way of a heart transformed by him.

Dietrich Bonhoeffer, the Lutheran pastor and martyr, taught Jesus' extraordinary way of the heart in the midst of his own suffering persecution by pro-Nazi 'German Christians'. He wrote his meditation on the forgiveness of enemies in 1937, the year the Gestapo closed the seminary he founded, with the arrest of twenty seven of his friends, pastors and students. Bonhoeffer was arrested in 1943 and executed in Flossenbürg concentration camp in 1945.

Jesus' call to us to be extraordinary [*perissos*] is found in his Sermon on the Mount, Matthew 5:43-48:

You have heard that it was said, "You shall love your neighbour and hate your enemy." But I say to you, love your enemies and pray for those who persecute you, so that you may be sons of your Father who is in heaven; for he makes his sun rise on the evil and on the good, and sends rain on the just and on the unjust. For if you love those who love you, what reward have you? Do not even the tax collectors do the same? And if you salute only your brethren, what more are you doing [*perissos*] than others? Do not even the Gentiles do the same? You, therefore, must be perfect, as your heavenly Father is perfect.

Bonhoeffer points out that Christians are called to be different from other men in our forgiveness of our enemies; Jesus calls us not to follow the expected way, but instead to be 'peculiar', 'unusual', 'extraordinary'. For Jesus the "hall-mark of the Christian is the 'extraordinary'." The Christian cannot live at the world's level, because he must always remember the 'extraordinary'. What is the 'extraordinary'?

It is unreserved love for our enemies, for the unloving and the unloved, love for our religious, political and personal adversaries. In every case it is the love which was fulfilled in the cross of Christ. What is the extraordinary? It is the love of Jesus

Christ himself, who went patiently and obediently to the cross – it is in fact the cross itself. The cross is the differential of the Christian religion, the power which enables the Christian to transcend the world and to win the victory. The *passio* in the love of the Crucified is the supreme expression of the 'extraordinary' quality of the Christian life.[25]

Jesus' extraordinary way of the heart

Bonhoeffer presents a checklist of Christian attitudes and behaviours that comprise Jesus' extraordinary way of the heart:

Love your enemies (*Mt* 5:44): Jesus commands us to not only show patience towards our enemy and refrain from a tit-for-tat response, but to actively show heart-felt loving service towards him. "If out of love for our brother we are willing to sacrifice goods, honour and life, we must be prepared to do the same for our enemy".[26]

Bless them that persecute you (*Lk* 6:28): Following Jesus' example on the cross we must respond to our enemies, curses with blessing. "We are ready to endure their curses so long as they redound to their blessing".[27]

Do good to those that hate you (*Lk* 6:27): It is not enough to love our enemies in thought and word, we must also show them we love them through our service. "As brother stands by brother in distress, binding up his wounds and soothing his pain, so let us show our love towards our enemy. There is no deeper distress to be found in the world, no pain more bitter than our enemies".[28]

Pray for those who mistreat you (*Lk* 6:28): Bonhoeffer calls this the "supreme demand" because when we pray for our enemies in the very act of mistreating us we are accepting their spiritual wellbeing as our responsibility:

> For if we pray for them, we are taking their distress and poverty, their guilt and perdition upon ourselves, and pleading to God for them. We are doing vicariously for them what they cannot do for themselves. Every insult they utter only serves to bind us more closely to God and them.[29]

By showing us how to love our enemies from the cross, Jesus is asking us to abandon the vicious cycle of hatred and revenge.

My mind agrees with Bonhoeffer, but I must admit that in my heart I remain conflicted by Our Lord's teaching on forgiving our enemies, because, as Bonhoeffer observes, part of me – my "old nature" – finds the prospect of loving, blessing, and praying for my enemies intolerably offensive, against justice, and intractably difficult. When I think of my enemies, or have anything to do with them, either my blood boils with anger or I feel a very cold rage that longs for revenge. How do I put off my old nature and put on the new nature of Our Lord Jesus Christ, true God and true man?

Bonhoeffer writes that when it comes to Jesus' teaching on rejecting the way of revenge it all boils down to this question – what do we value the most? Our right to justice, defended at all costs, or our exclusive adherence to Jesus no matter what? We can't have both. The refusal to forgive from the heart and the desire for revenge has no place in the extraordinary way of Jesus.

Our Lord calls us to share his Passion by accepting in our lives our own passion at the hands of our enemies. This doesn't mean pretending everything is OK when we are being bullied or persecuted. Jesus confronted evil, and he named evil for what it was:

> We are concerned not with evil in the abstract, but with the evil person. Jesus bluntly calls the evil person evil. If I am assailed, I am not to condone or justify aggression. Patient endurance of evil does not mean a recognition of its right. That is sheer sentimentality, and Jesus will have nothing to do with it. The shameful assault, the deed of violence and the act of exploitation are still evil.

The disciple must realise this, and bear witness to it as Jesus did, just because this is the only way evil can be met and overcome. The very fact that the evil which assaults him is unjustifiable makes it imperative that he should not resist it, but play it out and overcome it by patiently enduring the evil person. Suffering willingly endured is stronger than evil, it spells death to evil.[30]

I understand Bonhoeffer as meaning that if we act on our feelings of hatred and revenge we're no better than our enemies, because by doing so we validate and perpetuate the evil committed against us. Instead, Jesus calls us to break the vicious cycle of revenge by embracing his extraordinary way of the heart.

We know that Jesus' extraordinary way of forgiveness works. His victory on the cross, over sin, death and the devil, promises us that our rejection of hatred and revenge will be victorious. "The cross is the only power in the world which proves that suffering love can avenge and vanquish evil".[31]

I get frustrated when I find myself harbouring resentful, vengeful thoughts and fantasies in my heart. Despite knowing the truth of Jesus' teaching about forgiving our enemies and wanting to follow his commands, I find it so difficult to break this vicious cycle. To make matter worse, fresh offences and insults often trigger all the old resentments into action. Clearly I don't love Our Lord with all my heart, because I remain stubbornly attached to the ordinary ways of the hard heart. Every day I make a new beginning to be 'extraordinary' like Jesus, encouraged by occasional moments of grace that warm my heart and show me the right way to go.

The indwelling of God in our heart

Hearts hardened by rebellion against God and hatred of our fellow man can never be a dwelling place for his spirit (*Ezk* 36:27). But Jesus promises that those who follow his extraordinary way of the heart will become something even more marvellous – a dwelling place for the Most Holy Trinity:

"If a man loves me, he will keep my word, and my Father will love him, and we will come to him and make our home with him." (*Jn* 14:23)

Loving Jesus and keeping his commandments are the essential precondition for the indwelling of God in our hearts. As F J Moloney points out, priority is given to loving Jesus because, as Bonhoeffer reflected, those who love Jesus will want to keep his "word". In the Old Testament the Ten Commandments are referred to as the "words" of God, so Jesus' injunction that his disciples "keep his word" has the binding authority of the Ten Commandments.

The Greek word for "indwelling" is the same word used to describe the heavenly abode with the Father (Fr Raymond Brown). Here Jesus is promising that the Most Holy Trinity will make the heart into a little heaven for those who follow his extraordinary way.

St Paul also writes about the heart of the true disciple becoming the dwelling place of the Most Holy Trinity, in terms of the dwelling place of Christ and the Temple of the Holy Spirit:

> I pray that, according to the riches of his glory, he may grant that you may be strengthened in your inner being with power through his Spirit, and that Christ may dwell in your heart through faith, as you are being rooted and grounded in love. I pray that you may have the power to comprehend, with all the saints, what is the breadth and length and height and depth, and to know the love of Christ that surpasses knowledge, so that you may be filled with all the fullness of God. (*Ep* 3:16-19)

Christ's dwelling in the innermost centre of a person is a profound experience of divine love. It is the beginning of our eternal encounter with the God who is love.

The sweet fire

The Gospel of Luke gives an account of Our Lord affecting his disciples' hearts in such a profound way:

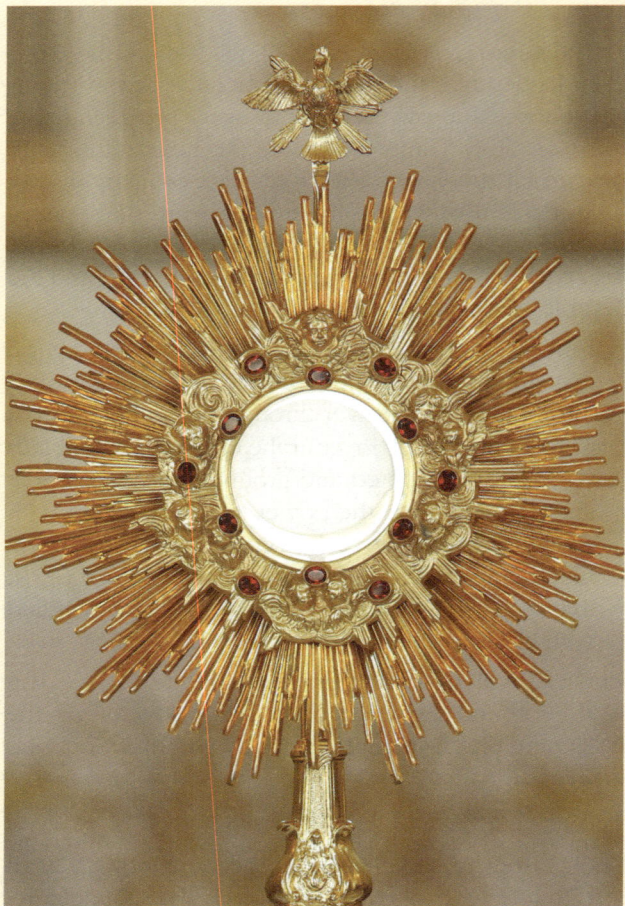

When he was at table with them, he took the bread
and blessed, and broke it, and gave it to them.
And their eyes were opened and they recognised
him; and he vanished out of their sight. They said
to each other, "Did not our hearts burn within us
while he talked to us on the road, while he opened
to us the Scriptures?" (*Lk* 24:30-32)

The Greek word translated as 'burn' or 'burning' –
"Did not our hearts burn within us" – is associated
with love, in the sense of 'burning with love', being
'consumed by love'. As they listened to the resurrected
Jesus explain his role in Salvation History through the
Scriptures their hearts 'burned' with love. Hearts that
had been "slow to believe" (*Lk* 24:25) burned with
love in the presence of the risen Christ.

Michael O'Brien, the Catholic author, refers to this
encounter with the love of God in the heart as the
"sweet fire", that we may experience, according to
the will and grace of God, during prayer, especially
after reception of Holy Communion and in adoration
before the Blessed Sacrament:

He felt it as a sweet fire that surrounded and
gradually filled his agony… The fire of Presence on
this altar was the embrace of total love; it burned
but did not consume. It gave joy, not pain. It did not
bind its creatures nor mutilate their flesh. It freed
them. It gave light. It consoled and it fed them.[32]

"...Holy Communion, when the sweet fire entered her flesh and radiated through all layers of her being. It was too much, it was too generous. But she drank and drank it and let him warm her through and through."[33]

The sweet fire is a gift of the living God, who grants it as a consolation or withholds it to encourage us to make the leap of pure faith. It is an unmerited gift dependent solely on the will of God. I think the sweet fire is one of the ways God's mysterious plan works out in our lives to enable us to become "partakers of the divine nature" (2 P 1:4).

Let Jesus heal your heart: prayer reflections

- God promises to place a new heart within us. Do I let Jesus heal my heart?

- How much have I put on the new nature of Jesus and forgiven others from my heart?

- Jesus tells us:
  - Love your enemies (*Mt* 5:44).
  - Bless them that persecute you (*Lk* 6:28).
  - Do good to those that hate you (*Lk* 6:27).
  - Pray for those who mistreat you (*Lk* 6:28).

- Do I try to break the vicious cycle of revenge?

- Jesus comes into our hearts in the "sweet fire" that burns with his presence. Do I wait trusting in quiet prayer and adoration for him to enter my heart?

Jesus, healer of my heart, stay with me in my need for I am broken hearted and need your healing. Gently take the heart of stone within me and make it into a heart of flesh. Ease the pain as you transform this heart of stone as I drop each resentment, each hurt, each thought of revenge. Protect and comfort me for I feel so weak and vulnerable with a heart of flesh. Fill me with your forgiveness so that I will be able to forgive. Amen.

Fr Seraphim Rose and the Tears of the Heart

One of the fundamental beliefs of the Catholic faith is that God has placed in the human heart the desire to be happy. This universal desire for happiness is of divine origin, "God has placed it in the human heart in order to draw man to the One who alone can fulfil it".[34] This desire for happiness is the main spring of man's response to God's initiative of Salvation History – it shapes our beginning and our end:

"The desire for God is written in the human heart, because man is created by God and for God; and God never ceases to draw man to himself. Only in God will he find the truth and happiness he never stops searching for".[35]

Jesus' Sermon on the Mount is the great guidebook to living happily. The Beatitudes, part of the Sermon of the Mount (*Mt* 5:3-12), address ways that make man "blessed"; bring him a happiness that is more than being cheerful (Cardinal Schönborn).

The Beatitudes succinctly describe Jesus' life – Jesus was humble, he mourned for the sin and cruelty around him, he was meek, he hungered and thirsted for justice, he was merciful, he was pure in heart, he was a peacemaker and he was persecuted, reviled and the subject of false accusations. Through the Beatitudes Jesus is saying that we will attain right and proper happiness – that is the fulfilment of our desire to find and see God – through following him along the way of the cross, through leading a life of self-giving love that shares in his death and resurrection. As a medieval proverb puts it, "The Way of the Cross is the Way of Light":

> The Beatitudes depict the countenance of Jesus Christ and portray his charity. They express the vocation of the faithful associated with the glory of his Passion and resurrection; they shed light on the actions and attitudes characteristic of the Christian life; they are the paradoxical promises that sustain hope in the midst of tribulations; they proclaim the blessings and rewards already secured, however dimly, for Christ's disciples; they have begun in the lives of the Virgin Mary and all the saints.[36]

Obviously, the Beatitudes exceed our natural expectations of what constitutes a happy life by identifying poverty, affliction and persecution as some of the ways to fulfilling our desire for happiness. This is shocking. However, if we truly believe that Jesus Christ, true God and true man, is the perfect man who fully reveals man to man himself,[37] then Jesus' life must be the pattern of how we ourselves live our lives.

Fr Seraphim Rose's journey to the centre of his heart

The life of Fr Seraphim Rose shows how living Jesus' extraordinary way of the heart transforms suffering into joy.

Thirty six years after his death Fr Seraphim Rose (1934-1982) remains a much loved monk throughout the Orthodox world due to his writings and recorded talks. But more than this Fr Seraphim is loved because he is a key figure in the rebirth of Orthodoxy in the Soviet Union behind the Iron Curtain. His writings were smuggled into the USSR and secretly copied and distributed by the thousands as *samizdat* (clandestine material banned by the KGB).

Seraphim Rose, born Eugene Rose, had not always been a Christian. Before his reception into the Russian Orthodox Church in 1962 Eugene was a nihilist and hedonist with homosexual tendencies, which he renounced on his conversion. Since his death he is recognised as a *Podvizhnik*, a Righteous Struggler, a way to sanctity characterised by the radical living of the Beatitudes, putting off the old man and putting on the extraordinary nature, "which is renewed after the image of him who created him" (*Col* 3:9-10).

Eugene was born in San Diego, California, into a middle-class family that was nominally Protestant. As a young boy, on his own initiative, he was baptised and confirmed in the Methodist ecclesial community, but during High School he lost interest in religion, preferring science and mathematics. Exceptionally intelligent, Eugene excelled academically, attaining a scholarship to one of America's best universities, Pomona College, known as the "Oxford of the Orange Grove". During his time at Pomona Eugene completely rejected Christianity:

> He had begun to hate the complacent, prosaic, consumer-orientated, middle-class culture in which he had been raised. Its idea of God, he felt, was shallow and provincial, not worthy of one who aspires to the highest reaches of the intellect; its religion was an unquestioning acceptance of facile answers by people who are afraid or actually unable to look deeper into the nature of things.[38]

Angry young man

With his rejection of Christianity and the 'American Dream' Eugene became an "angry young man", who explored the ultimate questions of life with increasing frustration, and a corresponding descent into alcohol abuse, and sexual immorality. He detested pretence and phoniness, obsessively seeking the true and the real while out-of-hand rejecting God.

Eugene was drawn to the work of the anti-Christian philosopher Friedrich Nietzsche (1844-1900), with whom he shared the experience of deep loneliness, bitterness and desperation. In 1956 the suicide of Eugene's friend, Kaizo Kubo, affected him deeply, increasing his sense of alienation and isolation. He said to a friend, "Each of us wears a mask…and no one knows what's behind it."[39]

Eugene came under the influence of Professor Alan Watts (1915-1973), a former Anglican priest, who had also rejected Christianity to become one of the leading Western experts in Zen Buddhism and an influential figure in the nascent New Age movement. Alan Watts' version of oriental religions made no moral demands on its adherents out of a conscious rejection of Christianity's sexual morality.

On graduating from Pomona, Eugene enrolled as a Masters student at Alan Watts' American Academy of Asian Studies at San Francisco. Among the people with whom he mixed he was encouraged to accept a "spirit of lawlessness" by engaging in acts of grave depravity. "As he stated in later years, this was the darkest, most miserable period in his life. Forbidden deeds, he said, had disgusted him even at the time he was committing them. They would precipitate long periods of depression afterwards". He sought to escape his guilt through hedonistic distractions, such as heavy drinking and gourmet eating.[40] A letter to a friend at that time also suggests that Eugene's conscience was troubling him:

> The punishment of sin is sin. Pain is the greatest blessing, for it awakens man from his self-hypnosis, the self-delusion that can take any earthly goal – be it crude, such as sex, food, comfort, or subtler, such as art, music, literature – as final. The desire for these things fails, and man becomes weary. Then: he fades away or kills himself; or he undertakes the path of deliverance, salvation…[41]

Christ transforms anger into love

Eugene's vehement hostility towards Christianity lessened as he allowed himself to read Christian authors such as Evelyn Underhill and Max Picard who critiqued modern society from the perspective of Christianity's perennial Tradition. His friendships with Orthodox Christian students on his course also brought him into contact with authentic Christianity. Though Eugene began to attend Orthodox services from 1957 onwards, he continued to see it as just one authentic religious tradition, along with some forms of Buddhism, Hinduism and Taoism. At the same time,

Eugene became critical of his former mentor Alan Watts, describing him as a "pseudo-religious preacher" who manufactured a pick-and-mix 'religion' to justify hedonistic self-indulgence.

Eugene's experience of the beauty and truth of the Orthodox Divine Liturgy eventually led him to encounter the Truth that he had long sought, Our Lord Jesus Christ, the Way and the Truth and the Life (*Jn* 14:6):

> With my exposure to Orthodoxy and to Orthodox people a new idea began to enter my awareness: that Truth was not just an abstract idea, sought and known by the mind, but was something personal – even a Person – sought and loved by the heart. And that was how I met Christ.[42]

Eugene was received into the Russian Orthodox Church in 1962, becoming a monk in 1968 and taking the name Seraphim two years later.

The wonders of a heart open to God

Until his conversion Fr Seraphim had zealously lived by the delusion of materialist secularism that truth could only be discovered by the scientific intellect's understanding of sense data. As an Orthodox Christian Fr Seraphim's eyes opened to the wonders of knowing truth through the heart:

Is there a special organ for receiving revelation from God? Yes, in a certain sense, there is such an organ, though usually we close it and do not let it open up: God's revelation is given to something called a loving heart… It is not first of all miracles that reveal God to men, but something about God that is revealed to a heart that is ready for it. This is what is meant by a "burning heart".[43]

Fr Seraphim discovered the biblical understanding of the role of the heart as the centre of consciousness and intelligence, and the source of knowledge and perception of the truth of things. He described the heart as the "organ that knows God":

"The Patristic teaching on pain of heart is one of the most important teachings for our days when 'head-knowledge' is so overemphasised at the expense of the proper development of emotional and spiritual life".[44]

The pain of the heart

Confronting his own personal history of serious sin, Fr Seraphim learned the Church's wisdom about the essential role contrition plays in the lifelong process of conversion. Fr Seraphim called this the "pain of the heart". Fr Jean Corbon describes contrition as experiencing "the baptism of tears, which cleanses it of its sins".[45] Fr Seraphim drew on his decades of existential suffering to describe the importance of the pain of the heart to grasp the truth of our lives:

"The right approach is found in a heart which tries to humble itself and simply knows that it is suffering, and that there somehow exists a higher truth which can not only help this suffering, but can bring it into a totally different dimension."[46]

The intense suffering of knowing our sin in the light of God's love purifies the heart, enabling us to achieve the fulfilment of our supernatural destiny, for only the pure of heart see God.

The prayer of the heart

The pain of the heart can be most experienced during prayer, when the voice of conscience and the grace of Christ enables us to see how our sins betray Christ and the harm that they have done to others and ourselves. Praying the orthodox prayer, the Jesus Prayer, inevitably leads to contrition, through the repetition of the simple words, "Lord Jesus Christ, Son of God, have mercy on me, a sinner". This prayer has been called "the Gospel in a sentence".

Fr Seraphim Rose taught the importance of praying the Jesus Prayer from the heart, not the mind, otherwise it will remain at the surface level of words and not transform our hard hearts. He related the following true story:

In San Francisco there was a person who got on fire with the idea of the Jesus Prayer. He began adding prayer to prayer, and finally came to, in the morning, five thousand. Right in the middle of the world, in the middle of the city, in the morning before doing anything else, before eating, he was able to say five thousand Jesus Prayers on the balcony, and he felt wonderfully refreshed and inspired. Then it happened one morning that somebody else came out right beneath the balcony and began busying himself and doing something while the person was saying his last thousand: and it so happened that this person was so put out by this that he ended up throwing dishes at him! How can you deal with a person occupying himself with the spiritual life, with the Jesus Prayer, when all of a sudden, while he is saying it, he is able to start throwing dishes? This means that inside him the passions are free, because he had some kind of deceived idea or opinion that he knew what was right for himself spiritually. He acted according to his opinion, but not soberly, not according to knowledge; and when the opportunity came, the passions came out.[47]

Fr Seraphim came to understand that if Christ did not dwell in our hearts then our practice of Christianity would come to nothing, but if Christ really did live in our hearts then we would be able to heal our relationship with God and others, and help others do the same.

Fr Seraphim taught that prayer from the pain of the heart, led to prayer with pain for other people:

> We should make the other's pain our own! We must love the other, must hurt for him, so that we can pray for him. We must come out, little by little, from our own self and begin to love, to hurt for other people as well, for our family first and then for the large family of Adam, of God.[48]

Orthodoxy of the heart

Hieromonk Damascene, Fr Seraphim's biographer, writes that through his deepening prayer Fr Seraphim became "a man of the heart", and a preacher of "Orthodoxy of the heart", insisting that the Faith had to be, first and foremost, lived from the heart, and not restricted to the mind and intellect.

> Orthodoxy is something first of all of the heart, not just the mind, something living and warm, not abstract and cold, something that is learned and practised in life, not just in school... The true faith in Christ is in the heart, and it is fruitful, humble, patient, loving, merciful, compassionate, hungering and thirsting for righteousness; it withdraws from worldly lusts and clings to God alone, strives and

seeks always for what is heavenly and eternal, struggles against every sin, and constantly seeks and begs help from God for this.[49]

Fr Seraphim understood that true faith is always expressed through a soft and warm heart. And allowing our hearts to become warm must be the first priority of our lives, by putting aside our "ordinary rationalistic mind" and putting on the mind of Christ (*1 Co* 2:16):

> The first priority is the heart, which must be soft and warm. If we do not have this warm heart, we must ask God to give it, trying ourselves to do those things by which we can acquire it. Most of all, we have to see that we have not got it – that we are cold. We will thereby not trust our reason and the conclusions of our logical mind, with regard to which we must be somewhat "loose". If we do this, entering into the sacramental life of the Church and receiving the grace of God, God himself will begin to illumine us.[50]

Fr Seraphim Rose and the tears of the heart: prayer reflections

- In grief, in disillusionment, in suffering which seeks distraction, we find only deeper grief, deeper disillusionment and deeper suffering. Yet God wills our happiness so that we are blessed in all things. Is my prayer a prayer from the heart, a belief that Jesus can bring happiness?

- We can approach things with 'logic' or a cold heart that is neither soft nor warm. Do I live with a warm and soft heart?

- True contrition comes from the heart when we can see the harm that we have done to others and ourselves. Am I contrite?

Lord, let my prayer transform my hard heart. Let me feel true contrition. Let my tears drop as dew to melt my heart and bring it to life again, soft and warm with your compassion. Amen.

How to Help the Healing
of your Heart

When Pope Benedict XVI visited the United Kingdom he invited school children gathered to meet him to choose to become saints. He spoke to the children conversationally, wearing a blue stole decorated with hearts. The Holy Father explained that it was very simple to make this choice to become saints:

> Happiness is something we all want, but one of the great tragedies in this world is that so many people never find it, because they look for it in the wrong places. The key to it is very simple – true happiness is to be found in God. We need to have the courage to place our deepest hopes in God alone, not in money, in a career, in worldly success, or in our relationships with others, but in God. Only he can satisfy the deepest needs of our hearts.

Not only does God love us with a depth and an intensity that we can scarcely begin to comprehend, but he invites us to respond to that love. You all know what it is like when you meet someone interesting and attractive, and you want to be that person's friend. You always hope they will find you interesting and attractive, and want to be your friend. God wants your friendship. And once you enter into friendship with God, everything in your life begins to change. As you come to know him better, you find you want to reflect something of his infinite goodness in your own life. You are attracted to the practice of virtue. You begin to see greed and selfishness and all the other sins for what they really are, destructive and dangerous tendencies that cause deep suffering and do great damage, and you want to avoid falling into that trap yourselves. You begin to feel compassion for people in difficulties and you are eager to do something to help them. You want to come to the aid of the poor and the hungry, you want to comfort the sorrowful, you want to be kind and generous. And once these things begin to matter to you, you are well on the way to becoming saints.[51]

It's never too late to make this choice in our own lives, and it will transform our relationships with those around us.

Choosing the Way

One of the earliest Christian texts, outside the New Testament, is the *Didache*, or *The Teaching of the Twelve Apostles* (circa AD 96). It seeks to help the reader understand that existence presents us with two choices, we can either choose the Way of Life, or we can choose the Way of Death, "There are two Ways, one of Life and one of Death, and there is a great difference between the two Ways." The Way of Life was accepting discipleship of the Lord, and the Way of Death included all forms of immorality and evil. In the early days of the Church Christianity was called the Way (*Ac* 19:23), because it was an extraordinary way of life, very distinct from ordinary life.

I have found this understanding of life as consisting of making choices between two ways very helpful in living as a Christian. When I'm having to choose how to respond to words or actions that upset me, or make me angry, I now have the habit of reflecting which action of response on my part will be the Way of Life and which the Way of Death.

In his novel *A Cry of Stone*, Michael O'Brien writes that we are daily faced with making the choice between following the "blessing-way" or following the "bile-fire" way. The bile-fire way is choosing to harbour in our hearts anger, resentment, hate, dreams of vengeance and enjoying violence and destruction; while the blessing-way is choosing forgiveness, love, compassion, upholding God's commandments, thinking the best of people, and thankfulness for the gifts of life.

In *A Cry of Stone*, Rose Wâbos, the central character, always seeks to follow the blessing-way. A native Canadian, Rose, accepts the suffering of life as essential to the blessing-way, reflecting on the mysterious actions of God:

> Why was he taking things away? Why was he giving her more pain in her back and in her heart? Does love do such things? She reminded herself that the love-fire always returned, and that in the hidden-way, the blessing-way, he was asking her to be part of his work. If he was allowing her to be smaller and poorer and to bear more suffering, he would use it for a good purpose, take it into the Big Sacrifice, and from there he would pour more healing into others.[52]

Often when I'm caught up in the heat of the moment and reacting with anger I remember the choice between the two ways, and this brings me back to myself, enabling me to act with love and forgiveness. My fundamental choice, my basic orientation in life, is to be part of Jesus' blessing-way.

Pondering the word of God

Another action that keeps me on the blessing-way is spending time reading and praying with Sacred Scripture. I've noticed that if I start the day pondering a passage of Scripture I'm more likely to have a good day, and respond to others with greater love and patience, than if I decide not to meditate on Scripture.

Pondering God's word changes our hearts. The word 'ponder' comes from the Latin word '*ponderare*' meaning 'to weigh', and now has the meaning of 'to think about something carefully', especially before making a decision or reaching a conclusion. St Luke tells us that Mary weighed up the wonder and mystery of the birth of her son and of finding him teaching in the Temple not in her mind, but in her heart (*Lk* 2:15-19; 2:51).

Different translations of the Bible use various words to describe Our Lady's contemplation of the word of God – "pondered", "treasured", "kept" and "stored up". This constellation of words is important to help us understand the role of our hearts in treasuring Jesus with Mary. As it says in the *Didache*, the Way of Life includes thanking almighty God for making the Holy Name of God a "tabernacle in our hearts". Fr Jean Corbon writes:

Prayer "to" Jesus is our way of genuinely entering into the liturgy of the heart, because when we call upon Jesus "in the Holy Spirit" (*1 Co* 12:3), we enter into the mystery of his holy name. Isn't that how he himself teaches us to begin our prayer: "May your name be holy"? Invocation of the name of Jesus is not an optional method… Rather it is the first movement of the Spirit in the heart of the Bride: the Bride's entire mission is fulfilled in Jesus, and if we enter into the name of the Lord, we are on the only road that leads to the Father.[53]

Recognising Jesus' lordship over our passions

One of my favourite prayers for my morning offering is a medieval devotion to the Five Precious Wounds of Christ. The climax of this prayer is the final clause, "My Crucified Jesus, I kiss the wound in thy Sacred Heart with sorrow deep and true, may every beat of my heart today be an act of love for you".

One of the reasons I find this prayer so powerful is that it expresses the union that exists between my own heart and the Sacred Heart of Jesus in a very physical way – the beating of my heart. This conveys the truth that, "by his incarnation the Son of God has united himself in some fashion with every man…loved with a human heart."[54]

Through my devotion to his Sacred Heart I am aware of this communion between my heart and Our Lord's heart: "He who is united to the Lord becomes one spirit with him" (*1 Co* 6:17). I don't want to harbour passions and emotions that are unworthy of this heart-to-heart communion with Our Lord.

The stylised image of Our Lord's Heart crowned with thorns and bearing the wound inflicted during his crucifixion also conveys the truth that Jesus is the Lord of our passions. As the Church Fathers put it "he came to share in our 'passion'". The heart is the seat and symbol of the passions, and when displayed on an image or statue of Our Lord it conveys the profound divine reality that through the incarnation God assumed human passions. Jesus' capacity for passions is essential to our redemption because "there can be no Passion without passions: suffering presupposes the ability to suffer, it presupposes the faculty of emotions"[55]:

> Jesus knew and loved us each and all during his life, his agony and his Passion, and gave himself up for each one of us: "The Son of God…loved me and gave himself for me." He has loved us all with a human heart. For this reason, the Sacred Heart of Jesus, pierced by our sins and for our salvation, "is quite rightly considered the chief sign and symbol of that…love with which the divine Redeemer

continually loves the eternal Father and all human beings" without exception.[56]

Pope Benedict XVI encouraged all Catholics to foster devotion to Jesus' Sacred Heart, writing that it has an "irreplaceable importance for our faith and for our life in love" because it is "totally orientated to the love of God who sacrificed himself for us".[57] To learn how to pray this devotion read the CTS booklets, *Devotion to the Sacred Heart* and *The Sacred Heart: A Pilgrim's Companion to Paray-le-Monial* by David Baldwin.

Finding God when life breaks your heart is to shift away from preoccupation with your own hurt, with your own brokenness, to look at Christ. In that desire to gaze on him, a healing comes which is not possible when focusing on yourself. The choice to follow the blessing-way is a renunciation of self that places your heart in the Sacred Heart of Jesus.

I am still on that journey from my head to my heart – alert to the voice of conscience, aware of benign anger, but trying not to succumb to malignant anger. I long to completely accept the extraordinary way of Jesus, so that at last I am able to forgive my enemies from my heart. And in those moments of sweet-fire on receiving Holy Communion, I rejoice in knowing the source and destination of the blessing-way, "the loving kindness of the heart of our God who visits us like the dawn from on high" (*Lk* 1:78-79).

How to help the healing of your heart: prayer reflections

- True happiness is to be found in Jesus when we have the courage to place our deepest hopes in God alone.

A practical approach to finding God when life breaks your heart:

- Regularly review your conscience – are you harbouring hate, resentment, malignant anger?

- Pray for:
  - healing
  - a deeper understanding of love
  - acceptance of Jesus' extraordinary way
  - for forgiveness of others from your heart.

- Surrender yourself to God.

- Abandon your hurt and your situation to Jesus for him to deal with when you cannot cope.

- Immerse yourself in the sacraments – Reconciliation and Holy Communion.

Devotion to the Five Precious Wounds of Christ

My Crucified Jesus, I kiss the wounds in thy Sacred Head with sorrow deep and true, may every thought of mine today be an act of love for you.

My Crucified Jesus, I kiss the wounds in thy Sacred Hands with sorrow deep and true, may every act of mine today be an act of love for you.

My Crucified Jesus, I kiss the wounds in thy Sacred Feet with sorrow deep and true, may every step I take today be an act of love for you.

My Crucified Jesus, I kiss the wounds in thy Sacred Shoulders with sorrow deep and true, may every cross I bear today be an act of love for you.

My Crucified Jesus, I kiss the wounds in thy Sacred Heart with sorrow deep and true, may every beat of my heart today be an act of love for you. Amen.

Endnotes

1. J R R Tolkien, *The Return of the King*, p. 310
2. Jordan Peterson, *The Psychological Significance of the Biblical Stories, Lecture II, Genesis I: Chaos and Order*
3. *Catechism of the Catholic Church* [*CCC*] 1764-1765
4. *CCC* 1768
5. Alastair V Campbell, *The Gospel of Anger*, p. 31
6. *Compendium of the Catechism of the Catholic Church*, 77
7. St Ignatius of Loyola, *The Spiritual Exercises*, 327
8. Fr José Antonio Fortea, *Interview with an Exorcist*, p. 50
9. Fr Jeremy Davies, *Exorcism*, pp. 26-27, CTS
10. Peter Kreeft, *Making Sense Out of Suffering*
11. Neal Lozano, *Abba's Heart*, p. 37
12. *CCC* 2563
13. Vatican II, *Gaudium et Spes*, 14
14. Bishop Kallistos Ware, *The Jesus Prayer*, pp. 35-36, CTS
15. C G Jung, *Memories, Dreams, Reflections*, p. 276
16. Xavier Léon-Dufour, *Dictionary of Biblical Theology*, p. 228
17. Walter Eichrodt, *Theology of the Old Testament*, vol 2, p. 143
18. Vatican II, *Gaudium et Spes*, 14
19. *CCC* 1776
20. *CCC* 1779
21. Fr Albert Gelin et al., *Sin in the Bible*, p. 22
22. *CCC* 1792
23. Vatican II, *Gaudium et Spes*, 22
24. Dietrich Bonhoeffer, *The Cost of Discipleship*, p. 132
25. Dietrich Bonhoeffer, ibid., p. 137
26. Ibid., p. 133
27. Ibid., p. 133
28. Ibid., p. 134
29. Ibid., p. 134
30. Ibid., p. 128

72

31 Ibid., p. 130
32 Michael D O'Brien, *Father Elijah*, pp. 192-193
33 Michael D O'Brien, *A Cry of Stone*, p. 395
34 *CCC* 1718
35 *CCC* 27
36 *CCC* 1717
37 Vatican II, *Gaudium et Spes*, 22
38 Hieromonk Damascene, *Father Seraphim Rose: His Life and Works*, p. 23
39 Hieromonk Damascene, ibid., p. 41
40 Ibid., p. 57
41 Ibid., p. 60
42 Ibid., p. 100
43 Fr Seraphim Rose, *God's Revelation to the Human Heart*, pp. 25, 22
44 Hieromonk Damascene, ibid., p. 472
45 Jean Corbon, *The Wellspring of Worship*, p. 213
46 Hieromonk Damascene, ibid., p. 471
47 Ibid., pp. 628-629
48 Ibid., p. 833
49 Fr Seraphim Rose, "Orthodoxy in America: its Historical Past and Present", *https://www.stxenia.org/files/history/ortham.html*
50 Fr Seraphim Rose, "Raising the Mind, Warming the Heart", *http://orthodoxinfo.com/praxis/rose_raising.aspx*
51 Pope Benedict's address to pupils, St Mary's University College, 2010
52 Michael O'Brien, *A Cry of Stone*, pp. 139-140
53 Jean Corbon, *The Wellspring of Worship*, pp. 209-210
54 Vatican II, *Gaudium et Spes*, 22
55 Joseph Cardinal Ratzinger, *Behold the Pierced One*, p. 57
56 *CCC* 478
57 Pope Benedict XVI, Letter on the Occasion of the 50th Anniversary of the encyclical, "Haurietis Aquas"

Hansel and Gretel

CHARACTERS IN ORDER OF APPEARANCE

WOODCUTTER
WOODCUTTER'S WIFE
HANSEL   ] Woodcutter's
GRETEL   ] Children
ALFREDO*   The Gipsy Leader
TOMMY   The Dame's Son
DAME DOTTY   The Dame
ROSE   The Dame's Daughter
ZIPPY   The Dame's Horse
THE PRINCE
WITCH HAZEL
FAIRY*
CHILD*   In Fairy Story
CHILD*   As a Mouse
FLUNKEY*

*These characters can also be chorus members.

Chorus as; Gipsies and Party Guests.

Dancers as; Gipsies, Fairies, Elves, Huntsmen, Birds.

Children as; Gipsies, Mice, Birds, Fairies, Toys.

SYNOPSIS OF SCENES

ACT 1

Scene 1   **A Clearing in the Forest**

Scene 2   **Inside the Woodcutter's Cottage**

Scene 3   **Another Part of the Dense Forest**

Scene 4   **The Forest Clearing**

Scene 5   **The Dense Forest Again**

ACT 2

Scene 1   **The Forest Clearing**

Scene 2   **Inside the Gingerbread Cottage**

Scene 3   **The Dense Forest**

Scene 4   **Ballroom of the Palace**

In addition several sub scenes are played on the apron in front of tabs or a cloth to facilitate scene changes and allow the action to flow.

Hansel and Gretel

ACT ONE

SCENE ONE

A CLEARING IN THE FOREST. FULL SET. Woodcutters cottage one side, with practical door. Front of Gipsy Caravan opposite, with steps up to entrance. See production notes at end of script. A sunny day

CHORUS OF GIPSIES, DANCERS & CHILDREN. A WANDERING MINSTREL (Fiddle player if possible, or miming)

MUSIC CUE 1

OPENING CHORUS AND DANCE. (see music suggestions in production notes) During number WOODCUTTER, WOODCUTTER'S WIFE, HANSEL AND GRETEL ENTER from cottage and stand admiring and clapping along with the routine. End of number all group around stage as ALFREDO, the Gipsy leader steps forward. (Alfredo is also a member of the chorus)

ALFREDO: Friends, friends! We have had a wonderful party, but there is some serious business to attend to, so before you all return to your caravans, may I call together the elders for a council meeting.

There are shouts of agreement and THREE CHORUS come forward to him

ALFREDO: Are we all met?
AN ELDER: No, Dame Dotty is not here.
ANOTHER: We can't have a meeting without her, the wise one.
ALFREDO: Where is she then?
CHORUS MEMBER: Here comes Tommy, he will know.

TOMMY, the Dame's son ENTERS

TOMMY: Hi everyone!
EVERYONE: Hi Tommy!
TOMMY: *(to audience)* Hi, kids!
AUDIENCE: Hi, Tommy.
TOMMY: Come on then, say hi to Tommy! When I say hi kids, I want you to shout hi, Tommy! Will you do that?
AUDIENCE: Yes!
TOMMY: Smashing! Then we'll all be friends. Now, after three... three! Hi, kids!
AUDIENCE: Hi, Tommy.

TOMMY: *(pulling a disappointed face)* What about the rest of you then? All the big people as well. Hi, kids!

AUDIENCE: Hi, Tommy!

TOMMY: Smashing! Great!

ALFREDO: Never mind all that, Tommy. Where's your mum, Dame Dotty?

TOMMY: She's had to gallop down to the village to get her lottery ticket.

ALFREDO: Did you say gallop? On her old horse, 'Zippy'?

TOMMY: Yes, Zippy's always dashing about somewhere. They'll be here soon, my sister Rose is with them.

ALFREDO: It's about time you got your mother a new young horse.

TOMMY: Oh I will when I get around to it.

CHORUS MEMBER: Here comes Dame Dotty now!

CHORUS: Hooray!

DAME DOTTY ENTERS, backwards, pulling the reigns of ZIPPY, a very old, tired Panto horse. Dame wears a heavily polka dotted dress. ROSE, the Dame's daughter is pushing the rear. A shopping basket hangs from the horse. They arrive centre stage

DAME: Come on, come on, come on!... Woah, Zippy!

The front part stops, but ROSE keeps pushing the rear part and they close up together, so horse is squashed and tall. Then ROSE gives a final shove and steam issues in a jet from ZIPPY'S mouth and ears

ROSE: *(laughing)* Poor old Zippy. He looks like a squeeze box.

DAME: Well, accordian to you.

TOMMY: What a nag!

DAME: What a nerve!

TOMMY: I mean the horse, ma. Not you.

DAME: Yes, I think it's time he was retired to graze.

ZIPPY nods his head sadly

EVERYONE: Aahh!

TOMMY: You mean put out to stud.

Zippy looks happy, nods vigorously, opens up quickly to full length and paws the ground with a back leg

ROSE: Did you do the lottery mother?

DAME: Oh yes.

TOMMY: Suppose you won the jackpot, what would you do about the begging letters?

DAME: I'd go on writing them.

ALFREDO: Now Dame Dotty, we've got to have a meeting of the elders council.

DAME: Okay, but not before I've given some sweets to my friends. Come on kids.

CHORUS CHILDREN run to her. She takes sweets from the basket on Zippy and hands them around

OPTIONAL - Dame can also throw wrapped sweets to audience. Zippy looks downcast

TOMMY: Hey ma, what about Zippy?
DAME: Ooh yes I forgot. There you are Zippy. *(feeds him a sweet)*

Zippy nods happily and munches. Children return to their 'parents' - All CHORUS, CHILDREN and DANCERS drift off. EXIT, EXCEPT 'ELDERS'

HANSEL, GRETEL,WOODCUTTER AND WIFE EXIT into cottage. One of Chorus leads ZIPPY off. ALFREDO goes up steps of caravan to address the others who gather around in a group: DAME, TOMMY, ROSE, THREE ELDERS

ALFREDO: Friends, Romanies and countrymen, lend me your ears.
DAME: Really Alfredo, you go from bard to verse.
ROSE: What's the matter, Alfredo?
ALFREDO: It's the Prince.
TOMMY: What is?
ALFREDO: I've had a message from the palace to say that the Prince is coming here to give us an address.
DAME: But we know where he lives.
ALFREDO: To talk to us!
DAME: Ah.
ROSE: The Prince! Coming here? Why?
ALFREDO: I don't know. I only hope that it's not to say that we have got to leave his land.
DAME: I'm getting tired of constantly being moved on.
TOMMY: We're not new age travellers.
DAME: No, I'm an old age traveller.
TOMMY: Ma, you're like a worn out Brillo pad.
DAME: How's that?
TOMMY: You're an old age pan shiner.
DAME: *(slapping him)* Cheeky!
TOMMY: Only joking ma.
DAME: You can make yourself useful. Go inside and put the kettle on.
TOMMY: It won't fit me, ma.

She slaps him again and TOMMY runs up steps past Alfredo and EXITS into caravan

DAME: While we're waiting you can all go inside the van and I'll make you a nice cup of Rosie Lee.
OTHERS: *(ad. lib)* Thanks Dame Dotty, We can do with a cuppa. *(etc.,)*

They begin to EXIT into caravan

ROSE: You're not going to read the tea cups again are you, ma?

DAME: No need. I know what's in store for you and Tommy. Tommy's going to get another clip round the ear, the little tinker, if he doesn't soon get work mending pots and pans.

ROSE: He will when he gets around to it.

DAME: And you will go on dreaming of marrying a rich handsome young man.

DAME follows the others into caravan. ROSE, now alone, sighs and sits on the steps

ROSE: So the Prince is coming here! Ma's right, I suppose one day my prince will come along. Just a nice ordinary chap.

MUSIC CUE 2

SONG, ROSE. (See music suggestions) Toward end of song PRINCE ENTERS unseen by Rose. He applauds at end

PRINCE: That was very charming my dear.

ROSE: Oh!

PRINCE: I'm sorry if I startled you.

ROSE: No, that's all right. I was daydreaming.

PRINCE: So I gathered. Let's hope that one day your mister right will have the good fortune to find you. Tell me, are you one of the gipsy band?

ROSE: Yes sir.

PRINCE: There was to be a meeting here at the edge of the forest.

ROSE: Yes, the others are waiting inside the caravan. I will tell them.

PRINCE: Thank you.

ROSE runs up caravan steps and EXITS

PRINCE: What a charming girl.

He wanders around the caravan inspecting it. Looking at one place in particular, he frowns. DAME ENTERS from caravan. She is excited and flustered. The Prince approaches her

PRINCE: Good day madam.

DAME curtsies and falls over backward. Prince helps her up

DAME: Oh, your mint imperial, you are very tasty. I mean tasteful.

PRINCE: Is this your caravan?

DAME: Yes. My humble home. Like me, past it's use by date.

PRINCE: I see it has suffered a little oxidisation.

DAME: Beg pardon?

PRINCE: Where your caravan has rusted.

DAME: Princes are not supposed to do the jokes.

PRINCE: And I wish I hadn't.

TOMMY, ROSE, ALFREDO AND ELDERS ENTER from caravan and group

PRINCE: Good day to you
OTHERS: Good day, sir.
ALFREDO: You wished to speak to us sir?
PRINCE: The fact of the matter is that partly due to my own foolishness I have lost a great deal of money. My palace is rapidly becoming a crumbling ruin.
TOMMY: A bit like my ma.
DAME: Do you mind! How did this come about, your worship?
PRINCE: I was cruelly tricked by a witch, who took most of my gold and jewels in exchange for inside information on the winning numbers of the lottery. And on a roll over week too!
ROSE: How did you know it was a witch?
PRINCE: She came in the guise of a talking cat.
DAME: Oh, Mystic Mog, eh?
TOMMY: And did she let the cat out of the bag?
PRINCE: Not a meow. And now I will never be able to repair my palace.
OTHERS: Aahh!
PRINCE: So my message to you is this - I will handsomely reward anyone who can remove this witch and return my treasure to me.
ALFREDO: I'm sure we will do our best sir, as you are so kind in allowing us to camp in your grounds.
ROSE: I know our Tommy will have a try.
TOMMY: Yes I will, the moment I can get around to it.
PRINCE: And so my friends I must leave you now. And thank you for your kind attention.
OTHERS: *(ad. lib)* Good day sir. Goodbye. *(etc.,)*

They bow to him. PRINCE strides OFF

DAME: Ooh, what a nice man. I wonder if Cilla could fix me a blind date with him?
TOMMY: She'd have to blindfold him first.
ROSE: Have you ever been on a blind date, Tommy?
TOMMY: Yes. I asked her if I could see her home, and she showed me a picture of it.
ROSE: *(sighing)* Oh ma, my heart is all a flutter. What can it be?
DAME: Probably those pickled onions you had for breakfast
ROSE: No, I think I'm in love with the Prince.
DAME: No harm in dreaming.
ALFREDO: We must get on with our work, Dame Dotty. See you later.

ALFREDO and ELDERS EXIT, exchanging farewells

TOMMY: Now then, ma, what's to do?
DAME: Well I don't want to keep moving around the country, and I'm fed up with making pegs and telling fortunes. I want to take up a new career.

TOMMY: So do I. I've had enough of being a tinker, mending pots and pans. I'd like to be a famous sausage maker. And on the other hand I think I'm cut out to be a brain surgeon,

ROSE: That's clever, sausages on one hand and brains on the other.

DAME: Oh, I'd give my right arm to be ambidextrous. I'd like to be a home help. You know, with a uniform and all.

TOMMY: You should clean up at that.

DAME: Well I'm handy around the house, and a good cook.

TOMMY: Yes, you're the only person I know who can burn water.

DAME: Anyway I'm going to have a go. I'll start by offering my services at that cottage over there.

TOMMY and **ROSE**; Good luck, ma.

Dame does a funny walk to cottage and knocks on door WOODCUTTER'S WIFE opens it

WIFE: Yes?

DAME: Good morning missus. Could you do with a little home help?

WIFE: Yes, but I'll never fit you in, you're too fat.

DAME: What a cheek. I'll have you know I'm a dab hand at dusting, a star at scrubbing and I gained honours at hoovering.

WIFE: But I'm pitiful at paying. We're broke.

DAME: That's no joke. I'm sorry I spoke.

WIFE shuts the door. DAME comes away disconsolately

TOMMY: Hard luck ma. I'll see if I can get an order to mend some pots and pans.

He goes to cottage and knocks door. WIFE opens it

WIFE: Yes?

TOMMY: I'd like to talk to you about old pots.

WIFE: My husband's out. He's gone chopping.

TOMMY: At Tesco's? *(or name local store)*

WIFE: No. Chopping, wood. He's a woodcutter.

TOMMY: I'm a tinker. I mend pots.

WIFE: Lots?

TOMMY: No, just the occasional jug. I'm no mug.

WIFE: Well I hope things pan out for you.

She slams the door on him. Tommy comes away unhappily

DAME: Hard luck son.

ROSE: I've always fancied being a maid in a big house. If only I could work in the Prince's palace.

DAME: You'll have to start somewhere humbler.

TOMMY: Hang on, there's someone coming.

WOODCUTTER ENTERS with Axe on his shoulder

ROSE: I'll ask this man.

She goes to him and they meet outside cottage

ROSE: Excuse me sir, I wonder if you need the services of a maid?
WOODCUTTER: I can't afford one I'm afraid.
ROSE: Have you any children sir?
WOODCUTER; Two. Hansel and Gretel.
ROSE: Then I must be on my mettle. I could serve you as an au-pair.
WOODCUTTER: Au- pair?
ROSE: Au- pair.

The cottage door flies open. WIFE is there

WIFE: Oh yeah!

She grabs Woodcutter by the ear and projects him through into the cottage and slams the door. Rose comes away sadly

ROSE: Oh dear!
DAME: That's that then.
TOMMY: What's to become of us, ma?
ROSE: There's no luck around here.
TOMMY: We could do with some of that lucky heather that the gipsies sell.
ROSE: We're gipsies.
TOMMY: So we are.
DAME: But I've never had the luck to find any. Anyway, you two run along. Your old ma will think of something.

TOMMY and ROSE EXIT

DAME: I could do with something to cheer myself up first.

She goes to caravan steps and sits. HANSEL and GRETEL ENTER from cottage, throwing a ball to one another. They quickly tire of this

HANSEL: I m tired of this.
GRETEL: So am I.

They sit down, fed up, leaning against the cottage or a tree. Dame has been watching them

DAME: What's the matter with you two?
BOTH: *(startled)* Oh! Who are you?
DAME: I'm Dotty.
HANSEL: Are you?

GRETEL: You don't look silly.
DAME: No, my name's Dotty. Dame Dotty. Who are you?
HANSEL: My name is Hansel.
GRETEL: And I am called Gretel.

Dame rises and moves to centre, Children rise and come to her

DAME: You don't look very cheerful.
HANSEL: Neither do you.
DAME: Then we'd better do something about it.
BOTH: What?
DAME: We could sing a song.
GRETEL: We don't like singing on our own.
DAME: Haven't you got any friends?
BOTH: No.
DAME: Our gipsy children will sing with you.
HANSEL: But they are not here.
DAME: I know a way of getting them. *(goes to one side and calls)* Would anyone like some free sweets?

There is the sound of children's excited voices off stage and CHILDREN RUN IN noisily from all directions. They ad lib 'Sweets? where? how?' etc.

DAME: All right! Simmer down!

The children go quiet

HANSEL and **GRETEL:** Wow! That worked quickly.
DAME: How did you get here so swiftly?
CHILD: We were waiting in the wings.
DAME: I see.
CHILD: How do we get the sweets?
DAME: You have to earn them by singing a song to cheer us up.
CHILD: What shall we sing?
DAME: How about... *(names chosen song)*

MUSIC CUE 3

SONG AND ROUTINE, HANSEL, GRETEL, CHILDREN & DAME. (see music suggestions). On second chorus, ZIPPY ENTERS and dances with them. Dame's basket hangs on him. Zippy takes a special bow at the end to cries of "Good Old Zippy", etc., Children crowd around Dame, ad libbing, asking for their sweets

DAME: Okay okay. Quieten down now!

She goes to her basket and mimes giving out sweets to all the children except Hansel and Gretel who stand watching. CHILDREN EXIT, skipping happily

DAME: My basket's empty now, Zippy.

Zippy locks downcast

DAME: Oh no, there's just one.

She mimes feeding it to him. Zippy nods happily and skips away

DAME: And don't forget to clean your teeth!

Zippy stops, turns and nods, grinning, then EXITS

DAME: There we are. I feel much happier now. *(to Hansel and Gretel)* Do you?
HANSEL: Yes, but we would have liked a sweet.

They join Dame downstage and the TABS CLOSE behind the three for remainder of scene while scene two, interior of cottage is set

DAME: Oh my dears! You didn't get a sweet?
BOTH: No. Dame Dotty.
DAME: Aahh! *(then to audience)* Come on, you can do better than that! All together... Aahh!
GRETEL: We don't mind. we don't usually get sweets.
DAME: What, never?
HANSEL: No, I'm afraid our father is very poor.
GRETEL: There's not much profit in woodcutting.
HANSEL: Besides, our stepmother never allows us treats.
DAME: My poor little chickens. Is your stepmother very strict?
BOTH: Yes.
DAME: Never mind. One day I am sure you will both be rich and famous.
HANSEL: How do you know?
DAME: We gipsies can foretell the future.
GRETEL: Can you really?
DAME: Yes, but only for others. It doesn't work for ourselves. Now you must run along. I have to go and find Tommy and Rose. Bye bye for now.
BOTH: Goodbye, Dame Dotty.

DAME EXITS one way. HANSEL and GRETEL EXIT opposite

END OF SCENE ONE

TABS OPEN ON INSET

SCENE TWO

INSIDE THE WOODCUTTER'S COTTAGE. A humble room, dimly lit. There is a table and chair. WOODCUTTER'S WIFE is at the table, mixing something in a bowl. She sighs and puts it down

WIFE: What can I do? There is just enough dough to make only one more loaf.

WOODCUTTER ENTERS wearily. Puts down his axe and slumps into the chair

WIFE: You look exhausted, husband.
WOODCUTTER: I have been working hard all day and with little result, for although I have cut and sawn much wood, no one seems to venture this way anymore to buy it. Only gipsies, and they cut their own wood.
WIFE: Then you must find other work.
WOODCUTTER: There is no other work. I am only skilled in this trade.
WIFE: But I must have money to buy more food. See, I have only sufficient dough here for one more loaf. There is nothing else in the house.

HANSEL and GRETEL arrive at the door, but Hansel stops Gretel from entering. They stand listening to rest of conversation

WOODCUTTER: Our first duty is to the children. Let them have the bread. Perhaps tomorrow I can carry some of my wood to the village and have more luck.
WIFE: If you don't eat you will have no strength to carry a heavy load to the village. If the children eat the bread, then we will starve.
WOODCUTTER: We must let the children have it. It doesn't matter about us.
WIFE: No. I don't agree. I have a plan.
WOODCUTTER: What plan?
WIFE: They will suffer less if we take them to the deepest part of the forest and leave them there. They will not be able to find their way back to the cottage and maybe someone will look after them. At least we shall be rid of them.
WOODCUTTER: That is a cruel and wicked plan. How could I leave my own children alone in the forest?
WIFE: You listen to me, husband, I know they are your children and not mine, but I'm telling you I have no intention of starving! First thing in the morning you take them away. Understand!
WOODCUTTER: But wife...
WIFE: No buts... just see to it. *(makes to exit taking the mixing bowl)*

WOODCUTTER rises and follows her, speaking

WOODCUTTER: It's not fair. You can't expect me to do this to my own children...
WIFE: Then I will do it myself!

THEY BOTH EXIT. HANSEL and GRETEL now enter room

GRETEL: *(close to tears)* Oh, Hansel, what do they mean by leaving us in the forest?

HANSEL: It's her, our stepmother. She is making father do it to save food.

GRETEL: But perhaps we shall be able to find our way back.

HANSEL: I don't see how.

GRETEL: We could starve in the forest, or be attacked by wild beasts... *(she cries)*

HANSEL: Don't cry Gretel, I will try to think of something.

GRETEL sits in the chair. HANSEL sits on edge of table

GRETEL: Nobody loves us.

HANSEL: I'm sure father does a bit.

GRETEL: I don't think anyone does.

MUSIC CUE 4

DUET, HANSEL and GRETEL. See music suggestions. At end of song they are beginning to fall asleep when a GROUP OF MICE ENTER

MUSIC CUE 5

MICE DANCE. CHILDREN. LIGHTING CUE. The mice do a dance routine in which the choreography shows them getting the attention of Hansel and Gretel and then miming picking up things and placing them in a line, after which two mice tiptoe back along the line of invisible objects. On reaching the other end they mime great joy on meeting the others and all jump happily up and down. MICE all then dance off, waving to Hansel and Gretel, and EXIT

HANSEL: Did you see that? The mice were showing us what to do!

GRETEL: What do you mean?

HANSEL: Well, like finding things to lay a trail.

GRETEL: Oh yes, they were going like this. *(she copies what the mice have done, miming placing things and stepping along the line)*

HANSEL: Like stepping stones.

GRETEL: That's it, a trail of stones!

HANSEL: Come on, let's gather some stones. I'll fill my pockets.

GRETEL: And then we must get quickly to bed.

BOTH run off. EXIT

TABS CLOSE TO END SCENE TWO

There is a walk across while the cottage inset is struck. WIFE ENTERS followed by GRETEL, and a little way behind, HANSEL who places a stone here and there as they cross and ALL EXIT

TABS OPEN on...

SCENE THREE

*ANOTHER PART OF THE FOREST. (See scenery production notes) WIFE ENTERS.
(In the cross over, and now she carries a bundle: bread inside a cloth) GRETEL
follows her*

WIFE: Come along Gretel, don't dawdle.
GRETEL: You hurry too much, and we have been round and round. We will get lost.
WIFE: Nonsense!

HANSEL ENTERS, takes stone from pocket, placing it on the ground

WIFE: What are you doing, Hansel?
HANSEL: Oh... I thought I saw a pretty butterfly.
WIFE: You keep lagging behind so.
HANSEL: Sorry.
GRETEL: Why have we come here?
WIFE: Your father has had to carry a heavy load to the village, so I thought I would take
you out for a treat. Come along.

*She continues across stage followed by Gretel. Hansel also follows, stopping to
place more stones*

GRETEL: I'm very tired.
WIFE: Oh, very well. This place will do.
HANSEL: Do for what?
WIFE: Why, for our picnic. We are going to have a picnic.
BOTH: Lovely!

*Wife undoes the bundle, producing two pieces of bread which she places on the
cloth on the ground near a tree on one side of the stage*

WIFE: Now you two sit here and have your bread. I am going on to collect some sticks
for home. I will come back to you quite soon.
HANSEL: But there is no bread for you.
WIFE: Never mind, I am not hungry. Goodbye. And enjoy your picnic.

WIFE EXITS. HANSEL and GRETEL sit by the tree

HANSEL: Are you hungry?
GRETEL: Not yet. Perhaps we should save it. Do you think she has really left us?
HANSEL: I don't know, but we can soon find our way home anyway. I have left the trail.
GRETEL: And she never saw!
HANSEL: Shall we play a game first?
GRETEL: Yes. What?
HANSEL: Hide and seek? Or chase?
GRETEL: No not in these woods, we might really get lost.
HANSEL: Ball then.

GRETEL: We haven't got one.
HANSEL: We can use a stone. I have one left in my pocket.
GRETEL: No I'm really too tired and worried to play games.
HANSEL: Yes I feel tired too, but I will look after you.
GRETEL: How long shall we stay here?
HANSEL: We had better go before nightfall. Let's eat our bread now.

They begin eating, gradually falling to sleep

MUSIC CUE 6

BALLET. DANCERS. (See music suggestions) Dancers as Sprites, Fairies or Elves. Choreography to depict them caring for the children, covering them with a blanket of leaves etc., Solo dance, Spirit of The Forest can be incorporated. LIGHTING CUE: During ballet lighting changes slowly to night. U/V sequence could be used. End of dance, GRETEL begins to stir. DANCERS EXIT. GRETEL wakes

GRETEL: Hansel, Hansel, wake up!

Hansel wakes and stretches

HANSEL: What is it?
GRETEL: It is night. I don't like the dark. I'm scared.
HANSEL: Don't worry, the moon is coming out and we can go home.

LIGHTING CUE; Moonlight comes in through the tree

HANSEL: *(rising)* Look, see how the stones shine in the moonlight! Come, Gretel.

He picks one up and it shines (luminous paint) HANSEL and GRETEL follow the stones, picking them up as they EXIT

TABS CLOSE on Scene three

Now another cross over, HANSEL and GRETEL cross the apron, following the trail, miming collecting stones

GRETEL: The trail goes round and round, Hansel.
HANSEL: Yes, it seems a long way, but we shall reach home.

THEY EXIT

TABS OPEN FOR SCENE 4

SCENE FOUR

THE FOREST CLEARING. As Scene One, with caravan and cottage. Two benches are set, one behind the other to seat NINE people. GIPSY CHILDREN are playing, singing and dancing. Lighting full, sunny day

MUSIC CUE 7

SONG AND DANCE. CHILDREN. On applause DAME ENTERS from Caravan in school teacher's cap and gown. She carries a handbell and the register. She clangs the bell loudly and then puts it down

DAME: School time! School time!

The children groan

Come along, you must have lessons if you want to be like me.
CHILD: But miss, we don't want to stay ignorant.
DAME: Sweet child! I don't know why they let kids into pantomimes. Take your places!

Children sit on the benches

NOTE: There MUST be FIVE children. Any extras must EXIT. If less than five, use Dancers

Right. First I must call the register. Hands up all those who are present

All five children put their hands up. Dame counts them

Now hands up all those who are absent.

One child puts a hand up

DAME: So you are absent are you?
CHILD: No miss, but Tommy and Rose are.
DAME: Oh yes, where have that naughty pair got to?
CHILD: Here they come now.

TOMMY and ROSE ENTER carrying satchels. Tommy wears short trousers and school cap. Rose wears ankle socks and school dress

TOMMY: *(to audience)* Hi kids!
AUDIENCE: Hi, Tommy!
TOMMY: Super!
DAME: Sit down. You're late.
TOMMY and **ROSE:** Sorry miss.

They sit on bench

DAME: Why are you late?
TOMMY: We were feeding the horse.
DAME: You should have brought a note from your mother.
ROSE: You are our mother.
DAME: That's a poor excuse.
TOMMY: You are a poor mother.
DAME: How dare you!
TOMMY: I mean you're not very rich. Anyway I feel silly going to school at my age.
DAME: You are never too old to learn. And if you don't pass the next exam I shall send you to university. *(or mention local school)*
TOMMY: Goody! I want to study to be a bone specialist.
ROSE: Well you've got the head for it.

WOODCUTTER'S WIFE ENTERS from cottage with HANSEL and GRETEL

WIFE: Excuse me.
TOMMY: Why, what have you done?
DAME: Tommy! What is it my dear?
WIFE: May I have a word?

Dame goes to her

DAME: Certainly. Which word would you like?
WIFE: These two naughty children stayed out nearly all night. I thought they were never coming home, I was very worried. They need a bit of discipline, so I wondered if they could join your class?
DAME: Why of course.
TOMMY: But don't expect them to learn anything.
DAME: Come along you two.
WIFE: Thank you. Now just behave yourselves.

She passes the children over to Dame and EXITS into cottage

DAME: Sit there on the bench.

Hansel and Gretel sit

Now then, what lesson shall we have?
PUPILS: Tell us a story.
DAME: No, we are going to do spelling and drawing.

Pupils all groan

And if you all do well I'll give you a treat.
PUPILS: Hooray!
DAME: Tommy, Rose, give out the boards.

Tommy and Rose take boards from their satchels and hand them out. Nine in all including their own. Boards can be about A 4 size and have a drawing on one side and a large letter of the alphabet on the other. In handing them out do not let audience see the drawings/letters

DAME: Now I want you all to draw a picture on one side of your board of your favourite food, and on the other side write the first letter of the name of your drawing. Understand?

PUPILS: Yes miss.

DAME: Right... begin.

They all begin to mime drawing

TOMMY: Please miss, I can't draw my favourite food.

DAME: Why not?

TOMMY: The paper's not big enough for a stick of rhubarb.

DAME: Then you'll have to choose something else.

TOMMY: What?

DAME: I don't know.

TOMMY: Then I'll ask my gang. *(goes to audience)* Will you all shout out your favourite food?

AUDIENCE shout names of food. Tommy pretends he cannot hear and encourages more shouting

Okay, that will do. I've got the message.

DAME: For goodness sake Tommy, when are you going to start drawing?

TOMMY: When I get around to it. *(sits and mimes drawing)*

DAME: Anyone finished yet?

PUPILS: We all have!

DAME: Lovely! Show me then.

All pupils except Tommy hold their pictures up toward audience, then turn them around to display the letters

They individually have large colourful pictures as follows: TOMATO/T. EGG/E. APPLE/A. MARMALADE/M. ICE CREAM/I. MARMITE/M. ORANGE/D. NUTS/N. DAME describes them to audience in any order

DAME: Very good indeed. Have you finished yet,Tommy?

TOMMY: Yes miss. *(holds up PIZZA/P)*

DAME: You have all done very well.

ROSE: What about our special treat then?

The others echo this

DAME: Okay. If you can make your letters spell one word, then that will be your treat.

All the pupils noisily get into a straight line facing audience, holding the letter sides up. The word spelled is P A N T O M I M E

DAME: That's made you smile. We are all going to the pantomime.
PUPILS: Hooray!

They now put the boards down and go into a song and dance routine

MUSIC CUE 8

SONG/DANCE. DAME. TOMMY. ROSE. HANSEL. GRETEL and FIVE PUPILS. (See music suggestions) At end of number;

DAME: Lovely. Off you go to play.

ALL EXIT Except Dame

I do like children. I was one myself a long time ago. And I like being a teacher, the children say funny things. I remember one child being late one morning and when I asked why, he told me that there were eight children in his family but the alarm was only set for seven. I asked little Johnnie if he could tell me where god is, and he said "yes miss, he's in our bathroom. Every morning my dad knocks on the door and calls, my god, are you still in there?" And then....

She is interrupted by WOODCUTTER'S WIFE who has ENTERED from cottage

WIFE: Pardon me, but can I have another word?
DAME: Certainly. Where's my dictionary? *(to audience)* Excuse me. *(goes to Wife)*
WIFE: I'm sorry to trouble you, but I am very worried. It's those two children of mine.
DAME: Hansel and Gretel?
WIFE: *(deviously)* Yes. They were naughty staying out all day and night, as I had promised to take them to visit a sick aunt who lives on the far side of the forest. I must take them today or the poor old soul will worry.
DAME: So what's the problem?
WIFE: I just can't go today, and my husband is too busy as well, and I was wondering, Dame Dotty, if you would be able to see them safely through the forest?
DAME: Of course I can chook. I'd love to go for a tramp in the woods.
WIFE: That's very kind of you Dame Dotty. I'll call them.
DAME: And I must get my walking things.

DAME EXITS into caravan. WIFE goes to where the children have exited and calls...

WIFE: Hansel! Gretel! Come here my dears! Drat it, where have those pesky children got to? Hansel! Gretel!

HANSEL and GRETEL ENTER nervously

WIFE: Come along! Why do you look like that? I have a treat for you. Dame Dotty is going to take you for a picnic.

GRETEL: Really?

WIFE: Really. So there is no need to be all silly and nervous.

HANSEL: And will she bring us back again?

WIFE: Why of course she will. Stay there and I will fetch the bread.

WIFE EXITS into cottage

GRETEL: Hansel, can we trust her? Suppose she wants to lose us again?

HANSEL: In that case she would take us herself.

GRETEL: That's true.

HANSEL: I'm sure we can trust Dame Dotty.

GRETEL: Yes of course we can.

WIFE ENTERS from cottage with a small round loaf

WIFE: Here we are my dears, here is your very last loaf... I mean my very last loaf, the only food in the house. But don't you worry my pretty ones, your father and I will manage.

HANSEL: Are you sure?

WIFE: *(annoyed)* Yes! Don't you want to enjoy yourselves?

DAME ENTERS from Caravan having removed cap and gown. She wears a bobble hat and big walking boots and carries a walking stick

DAME: Coo..ee! Let's go walkies. *(holds her feet up to show boots, then comes down steps)* I love walking in strange places. I like to go where the hand of man has never set foot. They say that travel broadens one.

WIFE: Then you must have done many journeys.

DAME: Now then!

WIFE: Sorry. Dame Dotty. Now all you have to do is escort the bra... the kiddies half way into the forest.

DAME: Well you can only go half way into a forest.

WIFE: How is that?

DAME: Because then you will be coming out again.

WIFE: What I mean is, you need only take them to the deepest, most impenetrable and dangerous part and leave them there. They will know what to do then.

DAME: You mean go on to their old aunties?

HANSEL and **GRETEL:** Auntie?

WIFE: Yes, yes, yes, I've explained all that to Dame Dotty. You must all get along quickly. Here is the bread for your picnic.

Hansel takes it

So good bye and good ridd... I mean, god go with you.

They all say goodbye. DAME takes the children's hands and they EXIT

WIFE watches them off

WIFE: He, he, he! That's the last I shall see of that troublesome twosome.

She moves upstage laughing and is EXITING into the cottage as TABS CLOSE for next scene

END OF SCENE FOUR

APRON SCENE follows while scene FIVE is set

MUSIC CUE 9

GIPSIES HUNTING MARCH AND SONG. (See music suggestions) ALFREDO ENTERS leading CHORUS of Gipsies. He brandishes a butterfly net and others have fishing rod, nets, a gun, bow and arrow, handcuffs, catapult etc. Items for catching the Witch. One searches with a spyglass. They do a routine, marching and singing. The hunting can be extended into audience if desired. End of number, back on stage...

ALFREDO: Friends, we must try to capture the Witch for the Prince.
GIPSY 1: But we have no idea where she lives.
GIPSY 2: Or what she looks like.
GIPSY 3: Or if she has a name.
ALFREDO: I hear that the Witch is called Hazel.
GIPSY: That's a sloppy name for a Witch.
ALFREDO: Well she's a pretty oily character. Come, let's press on through the forest.

MUSIC CUE 9a

REPRISE OF HUNTING MUSIC as CHORUS MARCH OFF singing

DAME, HANSEL and GRETEL ENTER.

DAME: It's a lovely day for a walk, children.
GRETEL: Yes, but I don't feel lovely. Can we stop a minute?
DAME: Why of course my chicken. Is something the matter?
HANSEL: It's our stepmother. She wants to get rid of us.
GRETEL: Because there is not enough money to feed us.
HANSEL: The idea is for us to get lost in the forest.
DAME: This can't be true surely?
GRETEL: It is. She did it the other day but Hansel was very clever leaving a trail of stones to follow back to the house.
DAME: What about your father?
HANSEL: He is too frightened of her to help.
DAME: But my dears, what can I do? I'm supposed to be seeing you on your way to your aunties.
HANSEL: We have no auntie. It's all a story.

DAME: The wicked woman. How can I help?

GRETEL: Can't we lay another trail back to the house?

HANSEL: If we keep coming back home she will realise that she can't just lose us.

DAME: That's true.

HANSEL: But I haven't any stones to put down this time.

GRETEL: What can we use?

DAME: How about the bread?

HANSEL: That's a good idea.

DAME: Give it to me.

She takes the bread, breaks a piece off and begins crumbling the crumbs into a line on the floor

GRETEL: Hooray! What a super idea.

Dame does a little dance around and then a funny walk off

DAME: Come on kids, follow me. Walk this way!

The children follow her, laughing and copying her funny walk as she continues laying the crumb trail. ALL EXIT

TABS OPEN on next scene.

SCENE FIVE

THE DENSE FOREST AGAIN. The same set as Scene 3. A bright day. SOUND OF POST HORN OR TRUMPET. DANCERS ENTER dressed as Huntsmen

MUSIC CUE 10

HUNTING DANCE. The huntsmen/women form a group at the end. On applause, PRINCE ENTERS

PRINCE: Good morrow my merry men and may we have excellent hunting. Leave me now, I wish a little quiet.

DANCERS bow to him and EXIT

PRINCE: *(to audience)* Well my friends, things are not looking good. There is no sign of anyone getting rid of that wicked Witch, and I don't know which way to turn. If only there were someone to share my life.

ROSE ENTERS singing to herself. Sees Prince

ROSE: Why sir, I beg your pardon. I did not intend to intrude. *(she curtsies)*

PRINCE: My dear, your intrusion is most welcome. I am in need of cheering.

ROSE: Well I'm not so happy myself.
PRINCE: How so?
ROSE: I can't get a job. Tommy can't get a job.
PRINCE: How about your mother, Dame Dotty. Is she well?
ROSE: Oh yes, and always confident about the future.
PRINCE: I wish that I were. And perhaps I would be if the right girl were to come along.
ROSE: And if only Mr Right would come along for me.

MUSIC CUE 11

DUET, PRINCE AND ROSE. (See music suggestions) On applause TOMMY ENTERS

TOMMY: *(to audience)* Hi kids!
AUDIENCE: Hi Tommy!
TOMMY: I thought I heard someone singing. Why, it's you, our Rose and, er, ah... Mr Prince! *(he bows low)*
PRINCE: Good day to you. *(he shakes Tommy's hand)*

Tommy winces and withdraws it

Sorry, did I hurt you?
TOMMY: Well I had an accident, burnt my fingers in boiling water. All my own fault, I should have felt the water before I put my fingers in it.
PRINCE: Well it never rains but what it pours.
ROSE: But it hasn't rained lately.
TOMMY: No, it only rained twice last week. First for three days and then for four.
PRINCE: Never mind the rain. Have you tracked down that Witch yet?
TOMMY: I will as soon as I get around to it.
ROSE: They say that she haunts this forest.
TOMMY: What? I'm getting out of here.
PRINCE: You can't do that. This may be your big chance.
TOMMY: I don't know that I want a big chance.
PRINCE: Are you a coward then?
TOMMY: I'm president of the coward's club.
ROSE: Do you really believe in ghosts and witches?
TOMMY: Not half.
PRINCE: There is one sure fire thing that will keep evil spirits away.
TOMMY: Not a photograph of Dame Bagwash! *(or name a local personality or member of parliament etc)*
PRINCE: Singing.
TOMMY: You're joking.
PRINCE: No I'm not that's your job.
ROSE: We'd better sing then.
PRINCE: What?
TOMMY: Er, how about... *(names chosen song)*
PRINCE: How does it go?
ROSE: Very badly when Tommy sings.
TOMMY: You're only jealous. They wanted me to be one of the three tenors.

ROSE: Your kind of tenors are ten a penny.
PRINCE: Let's sing.

MUSIC CUE 12

GHOST GAG MUSIC. TRIO. (See music suggestions) They stand in a line and sing Shortly a horrid Witch ENTERS. WITCH HAZEL. Use Green follow spot. She sidles up behind them

TOMMY: Just a minute, Stop, stop, stop, I think my gang are shouting something.

They stop singing

PRINCE: Shouting what?
TOMMY: Something about a Witch.
ROSE: Have you seen the Witch? Behind us?
PRINCE: The Witch is behind us?

The three look slowly round. At the same time the Witch comes beside them, then steps back again when the three look back to the audience

THE TRIO: *(ad. lib)* There's no one there. You're telling us fibs. There's no ghost. Let's sing again.

They begin the song again. The Witch comes to beside Prince and taps his shoulder. Prince and Witch meet face to face. Prince panics and runs off, chased by Witch. BOTH EXIT. TOMMY and ROSE continue singing until they realise that Prince is missing

ROSE: Hang on, Tommy, where's the Prince gone?
TOMMY: He must have run off.
ROSE: Not afraid the Witch might come, surely? And him a Prince!
TOMMY: Never mind him. We'll keep singing so the Witch won't bother us.

They start the song again. WITCH sidles on again, going behind them

TOMMY: Now what? The children are all shouting again.
BOTH: Witch? Did you say Witch? Where? Behind us? Oh no she isn't!
AUDIENCE: Oh yes she is!

Repeat as required

TOMMY: Alright, we'll go and look.

They plod round in a circle, the Witch falling in behind them, so not to be seen. Then the WITCH runs off. EXITS

BOTH: *(ad lib)* What a rotten lot you are. There was no Witch. We'd better sing again anyway.

They begin song again. WITCH ENTERS, going behind them

ROSE: Stop, Tommy, they're at it again. The Witch? Where?
AUDIENCE: Behind you.
TOMMY: There can't be a Witch. Singing keeps Witches away.
BOTH: There's no Witch. Oh no there isn't.
AUDIENCE: Oh yes there is!

Repeat as required

TOMMY: Okay, we'll take another look.

They circle again, looking, but in opposite direction. The Witch follows them round

BOTH: *(ad. lib)* Told you there was no Witch. etc etc. Let's get on with our song.

They begin song again. The Witch goes beside Rose and taps her shoulder. Rose and Witch come face to face. ROSE runs off screaming, chased by WITCH. BOTH EXIT. Tommy continues singing until he realises that Rose has gone. He feels the empty space next to him

TOMMY: Where's our Rose gone? What? The Witch? Did you say Witch? Ooh 'er, there must have been. I'd better keep singing. *(his knees knock violently but he starts the song again)*

WITCH ENTERS and tiptoes to Tommy, tapping him on the shoulder. Tommy and Witch come face to face. TOMMY runs off, scared. Witch cackles with laughter

DAME ENTERS scattering bread. Goes right up to Witch and looks her in the face. WITCH is so scared she screams and runs off. EXITS

DAME: What's the matter with her? Was it something I said? Come on kids, are you there?

HANSEL and GRETEL ENTER

DAME: The bread's gone a long way, there's not much left.
HANSEL: I think we've gone far enough. We can settle down here. You can go home Dame Dotty.
GRETEL: And we will follow the trail home in the morning.
HANSEL: She will never suspect that you helped us.
DAME: But there is very little for you to eat now.
HANSEL: Yes, that bread has a big hole in it.

DAME: That's because it's wholemeal. Your mum should have made one of those long sticks with "nowt taken out".

HANSEL: That would have been mother's pride.

GRETEL: Don't call her mother.

HANSEL: I wish you could be our mother, Dame Dotty.

DAME: So do I my pigeons. But perhaps I can be your honorary auntie, seeing as you haven't got one.

BOTH: Yes!

DAME: Well a kind auntie wouldn't abandon you in a forest.

GRETEL: But you have to or you will be in trouble.

HANSEL: We will be alright. Don't worry. We will find our way back home at daybreak.

DAME: Very well my dears. Sleep tight...

BOTH: Nighty, nighty.

DAME: Pyjama, pyjama! *(gives them the remains of bread and EXITS)*

Lighting begins slow dim. Hansel and Gretel settle at the foot of a tree and begin to eat the bread, They yawn, rub their eyes and soon go to sleep

MUSIC CUE 13

BIRD BALLET. DANCERS/CHILDREN. DANCERS/CHILDREN ENTER as birds, flying movement around stage. Choreography depicts them finding Hansel and Gretel, taking remains of bread from their hands, then discovering the bread trail, miming eating it. One by one they pick up and follow the trail, EXITING. The final bird turning, rubbing a full tummy and waving to audience and the sleeping pair. Music continues as night falls into moonlight

MUSIC CUE 14

OFFSTAGE CHORAL BACKGROUND. CHORUS. To highlight mystical feel. EFFECT: Smoke machine, mist rolling in upstage during which the Witch's Gingerbread Cottage Flat travels on. Alternatively use lighting change. It should appear as if by magic. See production notes. Lighting Change: Dawn breaks, slowly up to full. Hansel and Gretel stretch and awake. Then rise. Background music fades out

HANSEL: Come Gretel, it is dawn.

He takes her hand and they go to where they think the trail starts

GRETEL: Where are the breadcrumbs?

HANSEL: I don't know. The trail has disappeared! All the bread has gone! Which way should we go?

GRETEL: Perhaps we have started in the wrong place.

They search about but cannot find start of trail

GRETEL: What has happened Hansel?

HANSEL: I don't know, I don't know.

ONE CHILD as a BIRD ENTERS, weaving around the stage, smiling and rubbing a full tummy. Then EXITS

HANSEL: Look, the bird dropped something.

They run to a spot

GRETEL: A tiny piece of bread!
HANSEL: That's it! The birds have pecked up all the bread!
GRETEL: We shall never find our way home now.
HANSEL: And I am so hungry.
GRETEL: Me too.
HANSEL: Gretel, look, over there.

They see the Witch's cottage

GRETEL: A cottage! But there was no cottage there when we went to sleep. How strange.

They move to it

HANSEL: What a funny house. It looks good enough to eat.
GRETEL: It's made of gingerbread!
HANSEL: And cakes!
GRETEL: And sweets! Now we can eat all we want.

They start to pull small pieces off the cottage, to eat them. The cottage door swings open. WITCH'S voice calls from inside.

WITCH: Come inside my pretties!

Hansel and Gretel look at one another, unsure what to do

MUSIC CUE 15

DRAMATIC CURTAIN MUSIC. The children are tentatively about to enter as the music swells and...

THE CURTAIN FALLS ON ACT ONE

ACT TWO

SCENE ONE

THE FOREST CLEARING. A bright sunny day

MUSIC CUE 16

SONG & MOVEMENT. GIPSY CHORUS. (See music suggestions) At end of number

ALFREDO: Friends, gather around. Our children and young people have devised a fairy story for your entertainment and enlightenment. Please welcome the Good Fairy.

FAIRY ENTERS. Probably the senior dancer, She curtsies to chorus who ring the stage as an audience

FAIRY: Good morrow friends. I come this day to relate to you a story of my fairy clan. This fable has a moral which I bid you all to heed. Once upon a time as Christmas approached, a child sat upon a grassy mound to watch his father's sheep as they grazed...

A CHILD ENTERS, looks around and then sits on the stage looking puzzled. He does not see the Fairy

CHILD: I wonder... which way is fairyland? Father Christmas comes from fairyland and I don't know which way to look. If only I could visit fairyland. *(cups head in hands)*
FAIRY: *(to audience)* But only good children may visit fairyland.

MUSIC CUE 17

Bright 'PAN PIPE' music. The child rises and looks around, attracted by the music

CHILD: Music? And what is this I see? A circle of lush grass and mushrooms. And over here another. Fairy rings! The spot where the fair folk dance!

A GROUP OF FAIRIES ENTER. (3 or 4) They move into a circle and dance to the pipe music. Shortly they beckon to the child who cautiously advances. He is snatched into the ring and joins the dance

MORE FAIRY DANCERS ENTER with garlands, flowers, fruit baskets and golden goblets

A fountain (Not practical, just a decorative bowl on a pedestal) is placed on. All gather around the child who is fussed over, garlanded and fed

The dance stops and the child looks in wonder

CHILD: Where am I?

FAIRY: You are in fairyland.

CHILD: Fairyland! It's wonderful. I like it here.

FAIRY: Then you may stay.

CHILD: Forever?

FAIRY: On one condition. That you do not drink from yonder magic fountain, or you will dilute our powers. Is it a bargain?

CHILD: Oh yes!

FAIRY: You promise?

CHILD: Cross my heart.

FAIRY: Then may the festivities continue!

THE MUSIC & DANCE Re-commences. The Fairy may do a solo. After a while the fairies grow tired, the music slows. They float to the ground and settle to sleep. The music fades and stops. The Child who has watched the dance waits until quite sure they all sleep and is drawn to the fountain. He cannot resist plunging his hands in to scoop up and drink the water

At once there is pandemonium. The fairies jump up, scream and chase the child threateningly in circles. The fountain and all props are run off and the FAIRIES (except leader) EXIT, distraught. The Child continues to circle alone until dropping at the spot where he had first sat, and holds his head in his hands. After a pause the child rises and searches for a fairy ring

CHILD: The fairy rings have all disappeared. *(walks sadly off. EXITS)*

FAIRY: And so my friends, because he broke his promise my fairy clan became poor, losing much of our power. Father Christmas could not find his way to the child's house and the child never saw fairyland again. *(she curtsies to the 'audience')*

The CAST of the Fairy Tale ENTER, take a bow to the on stage audience and EXIT. DAME ENTERS and speaks to Alfredo

DAME: Is this the way to fairyland?

ALFREDO: Hello Dame Dotty. You've just missed the show.

DAME: All the children?

ALFREDO: Yes it was very good.

DAME: Did Hansel and Gretel take part?

ALFREDO: No.

DAME: Has anyone seen Hansel and Gretel?

CHORUS: *(ad. lib)* No. Not a sign. Sorry. etc.

DAME: They should be back by now.

WOODCUTTER'S WIFE ENTERS from cottage. Seeing the crowd she makes to exit quickly through the forest. Dame sees her

DAME: Excuse me Mrs, er, thing, Mrs Wood.

WIFE: Yes?

DAME: Are the kiddies back home?

WIFE: What? Sorry, I'm in a hurry.

DAME: Young Hansel and Gretel. Are they back from their aunties?

WIFE: Oh, er, yes... no, not yet.

DAME: But they've been out all night and most of the day. Aren't you worried?

WIFE: Well, yes, yes of course I'm worried.

ALFREDO: What's the problem?

DAME: I took them half way through the forest yesterday so that they could visit an aunt.

WIFE: And the scallywags haven't come home yet.

ALFREDO: Perhaps we should search for them. The forest can be dangerous.

WIFE: I'm sure they will be alright.

DAME: You can't mean that. I think we should go and look for them.

CHORUS: *(ad. lib)* Yes we'll help. etc.

WIFE: No, really. I don't want you to put yourselves out.

DAME: Suppose that wicked Witch has trapped them!

ALFREDO: Come on everyone, let's find Hansel and Gretel. Spread out in different directions.

ALFREDO and CHORUS EXIT

DAME: Don't you worry missus, your youngsters will soon be found.

WIFE: Hugh! I shall look forward to that!

WIFE marches off EXITS

Terrible woman. Fancy not liking children. Those poor kiddies must really have got lost. I should never have left them.

TOMMY ENTERS carrying a bulging carrier bag

TOMMY: Hi kids!

AUDIENCE: Hi Tommy!

TOMMY: Hi ma!

DAME: What's in your bag?

TOMMY: Some very pleasant pheasant.

DAME: Will you give me one of them?

TOMMY: No.

DAME: If I guess how many you've got in your bag, will you give me one?

TOMMY: Okay. In fact if you guess correctly I'll give you BOTH.

DAME: Er,... Five.

TOMMY: Sorry. The answer's three.

DAME: Darn it. Anyway, Tommy I'm really worried about Hansel and Gretel. Our friends have all gone in search of them.

TOMMY: Shall we go too, ma?

DAME: Yes, but I can't walk as fast as them.

TOMMY: Then you should go by horseback.

DAME: Zippy you mean?

TOMMY: I'll go and fetch him.

TOMMY EXITS. Dame comes downstage onto apron. TABS CLOSE behind her for interior of Gingerbread cottage to be set

DAME: I'm not too sure about this. I can walk faster than Zippy when the wind's behind me.

Tommy's voice is heard off stage urging Zippy. HE ENTERS leading ZIPPY who is very slow and sad

TOMMY: Come on old boy, best foot forward.

Zippy stops and examines each front hoof and then places one of them forward

Is that your best foot?

Zippy nods

DAME: Aren't you feeling too well, Zippy?

Zippy shakes his head

DAME: Ahh! Zippy's poorly. Ahh!
AUDIENCE: Ahh!
DAME: Come on, he's poorlier than that.
AUDIENCE: Aaahh!
DAME: What's the matter then?

She holds her ear close to Zippy's mouth and he mimes speaking

DAME: He says he's got a cold. He's feeling a little hoarse.
TOMMY: We'd better take him to the vet.

Zippy shudders and shakes his head

DAME: You mustn't mention that name to him. He gets really upset.
TOMMY: Sorry. We could give him one of the vet's pills.

Zippy shudders, stamps his feet and shakes his head

TOMMY: Sorry. I didn't mean to mention the vet.

Zippy reacts again

DAME: Where are the pills?
TOMMY: I happen to have them here in my bag.
DAME: Along with the pleasant pheasant?
TOMMY: Yes.
DAME: How fortunate.

TOMMY: It was the director's idea. He couldn't afford another carrier bag. *(produces a huge pill. Brightly coloured tennis ball)*

Zippy reacts, backing away

TOMMY: Sorry Zippy, not that one. *(replaces it with a table tennis ball)*
DAME: It will make you ever so better, Zippy.
TOMMY: You'll be able to gallop again.

He tries to put the ball into Zippy's mouth but Zippy shakes his head and keeps mouth firmly shut

DAME: Let me try. *(she tries, with the same result)* I know, we need the tube.

Zippy is worried

TOMMY: I have it in the bag.
DAME: Would you believe it!

Tommy removes a long rubber tube with a funnel on one end

DAME: How does that work?
TOMMY: Well I put a sugar lump in the funnel and put the tube in Zippy's mouth and blow down the funnel, so the sugar lump goes into his mouth. When Zippy is enjoying the sugar lump I blow the pill into his mouth.
DAME: And where are the sugar lumps?
BOTH: In the carrier bag!
TOMMY: Come on Zippy, have a sugar lump. *(mimes putting a sugar lump in the funnel, puts the tube in Zippy's mouth, then puts the funnel end to his own mouth)* One... two... three...

He blows hard. Zippy swallows hard and munches happily

TOMMY: Good boy. Now, have another sugar lump.

He winks at the audience, shows them the table tennis ball, placing it carefully into the funnel

One... two... three...

Zippy blows hard and Tommy chokes, dropping the tube. Dame laughs heartily, so does Zippy as Tommy holds his throat and appears to swallow the ball. Suddenly Tommy neighs like a horse and starts to gallop up and down. TOMMY EXITS galloping. Dame, laughing, takes Zippy's reign and leads him off

TABS open on Scene two

SCENE TWO

INSIDE THE GINGERBREAD COTTAGE. Inset. See production notes. There is a cage large enough for Hansel to sit in. A stove with an oven door large enough for the Witch to get through. A table and two chairs. HANSEL and GRETEL stand just inside the door looking apprehensive. WITCH HAZEL is putting on her most welcoming smile

WITCH: Come my pretties, welcome to my humble home. I vow you have never seen a house as sweet as mine.

HANSEL: No indeed.

GRETEL: It's good enough to eat.

WITCH: So you are... I mean so it is. Little children are always tempted.

HANSEL: Have you got children then?

WITCH: I'm afraid not my dear. But I do love them, and I am so happy to have lured... I mean that you have chosen to visit me.

GRETEL: Well we just stumbled upon your cottage really.

WITCH: How clever of me. Of you I mean. What were you doing in this part of the forest?

HANSEL: Our stepmother wants to be rid of us and planned for us to be lost.

WITCH: Then she won't miss you!

HANSEL: What do you mean?

WITCH: I mean, how wicked she must be. Have you been in the forest long?

GRETEL: All night.

WITCH: All night! Then you must be very hungry.

BOTH: Oh yes!

WITCH: Yes you do look too skinny to make a good meal. I mean you look ill nourished, especially you boy. What is your name?

HANSEL: Hansel, marm.

WITCH: A singular name. And you can call me Hazel. Your kind aunt Hazel.

GRETEL: So we do have an aunt after all.

HANSEL: Hazel? Where have I heard that name before?

WITCH: Never mind that. And you girl, what are you called?

GRETEL: Gretel, if you please.

WITCH: Oh yes, you please me very much, sweet child. *(aside)* ... She will make a fine meal. But first a little look around my tasty home. See, here is my special stove, big enough to cook girls... I mean grills. Kiddies... I mean kidneys... and steak. Steak and kidney.

GRETEL: That sounds scrumptious.

WITCH: And see here, this lovely play house. *(she indicates the cage)* Now you look like an adventurous boy, Hansel. Have a look inside. *(she puts a hand on his shoulder in encouragement)*

Hansel ventures into the cage. The Witch quickly closes the door, turns a large key in the lock and puts the key in her pocket

GRETEL: What are you doing?

HANSEL: Why have you locked the door?

The Witch changes from nice to horrid, speaking to Hansel

WITCH: *(cackling shrilly)*   Hee, hee, hee, hee, my little scrap,
                                   You have fallen into my trap!
                                   You greedily wanted to eat my house,
                                   And now I've caught you like a mouse.
                                   I'll feed you till you are plump and tender,
                                   So I can go on an eating bender.
                                   I'll boil you with dumplings, gravy and onions,
                                   To appease my appetite for tasty young 'uns!
                                   Hee, hee, hee, hee!

Hansel cowers in the cage. Gretel screams and attacks the Witch who holds her off. Gretel struggles but cannot get free

WITCH: Struggle as much as you want my dear,
                                   For your fate, like your brother, is sealed I fear.
                                   You will cook and feed him dishes,
                                   To make him fat and fulfil my wishes,
                                   And when I have munched and chewed him through,
                                   I'll sharpen my knife and fork for you!
                                   Hee, hee, hee, hee!

The WITCH frog marches GRETEL off, kicking and crying. Hansel cowers in the cage very afraid. LIGHTING CUE: Lights dim to blackout to denote passage of time. PAUSE. Then lights slowly back up

GRETEL ENTERS with a food bowl and goes to the cage

GRETEL: Dear Hansel, I have food for you. The Witch made me cook it.
HANSEL: What is it?
GRETEL: Nice chicken.
HANSEL: I'm very hungry, but I'm afraid to eat, for if I get fat then she will eat me.
GRETEL: Yet you must keep up your strength.
HANSEL: Yes, so that I can find a way of getting out of here.
GRETEL: Why does everybody hate us?
HANSEL: I don't think everybody does, but it does feel as though it is just you and me against the world. Wouldn't it be lovely to have a warm comfortable home?

MUSIC CUE 18

DUET, HANSEL and GRETEL. (See music suggestions) After song, Witch's voice heard

WITCH: *(off)* Gretel! Gretel you little wretch, come here at once!

GRETEL EXITS hurriedly. HANSEL looks at the food

HANSEL: I will eat... but I have an idea! *(starts to eat)*

LIGHTING CUE: Lights fade to blackout, pause, and then return as before. Hansel is holding up a chicken bone and looking at it. WITCH ENTERS, hobbles to the cage and peers in with her bad eyes

WITCH: Here, lazybones. You have eaten a lot of food. Let me feel you so I can tell whether you are ready for my dinner.

Hansel pushes the chicken bone through the bars. The Witch feels it

Bah! Your finger is just as skinny as ever. I shall have to wait another day. Drat it, where's that girl? *(moves away to exit)* Gretel! More food... prepare more food...

As she EXITS, Hansel holds up the bone and laughs loudly

HANSEL: Ha, ha, ha, ha, the chicken bone!

TABS CLOSE on the scene

Apron scene follows

DAME ENTERS on apron leading ZIPPY

DAME: Oh dear, Zippy, I'm just about done in. I don't think we shall ever find Hansel and Gretel. I only hope the wicked witch hasn't got them.

Zippy nods. TOMMY and ROSE ENTER from the opposite side

TOMMY: Hi kids!
AUDIENCE: Hi Tommy!
ROSE: Hello ma, any luck?
DAME: I'm afraid not.
TOMMY: That reminds me of a joke. Do you want to hear it?
DAME and **ROSE:** No!
TOMMY: Okay. There was a piece of string that couldn't get served in a bar, and complained to the barman. Are you a piece of string? asked the barman. No, was the reply. I'm afraid knot.
DAME: You slipped that one in didn't you, Tommy. Let's get on with the plot.
TOMMY: I didn't think you were coming on the search, our Rose. You were searching for a job.
ROSE: Well I ran out of steam.
TOMMY: Oh, you tried for a job in the laundry then?
DAME: I worked in a laundry once. Ironing .
TOMMY: One of the press gang, eh?
DAME: Yes. And I'll have you know I was very popular. They wanted to nominate me for Miss World.
TOMMY: Yes, Miss Carpet World.

Dame slaps him

ROSE: That's enough jesting.

Zippy nods violently

TOMMY: You needn't agree, you're the biggest joke around here.

Zippy looks downcast

OTHERS: Aahh!
ROSE: Hang on, there's someone coming.

THE WOODCUTTER ENTERS, looking worried

DAME: Hello Mr Woodcutter, you look very worried.
WOODCUTTER: I am, I got back from a hard day in the village to find my dear Hansel and Gretel missing and my wife feeling ill.
DAME: Your wife ill? What's the matter?
WOODCUTTER: I think she's got the flu.
TOMMY: Yes I saw her sweeping the chimney.

Dame slaps him

TOMMY: Sorry.
DAME: If she's got a headache tell her to thrust her head through a window and the pane will disappear.
WOODCUTTER: I think she's suffering from remorse.
DAME: That's nasty. Worse than lumbago.
WOODCUTTER: No, it's self pity about what she has done to the the children.
DAME: I should think so, the wicked woman.
WOODCUTTER: And I am desperate to find my children. It's really all my fault.
ROSE: Come on then, we must continue the search. However long it may take.
WOODCUTTER: Thank you all.
TOMMY: Let's split up again.

DAME leads ZIPPY OFF followed by ROSE. TOMMY and WOODCUTTER EXIT the other way

TABS OPEN again on the Witch's Cottage Interior. HANSEL is still in the cage, the WITCH beside it

WITCH: Put out your finger again, boy.

Hansel pokes the chicken bone out. The Witch, screwing up her eyes, feel it

WITCH: Still as bony as ever! Wretched brat! The more I feed him the thinner he seems to get. Where's that girl? Gretel! Gretel come here at once.

GRETEL ENTERS, very tired, carrying a birch broom

WITCH: Have you swept the yard?
GRETEL: Yes.
WITCH: And chopped the logs?
GRETEL: Yes. And fed Hansel again and again.
WITCH: Well no more. My cupboard is almost bare of that horrid food you mortals eat. And I am ravenous. I will wait no longer. Bony or not, Hansel must go to the pot!
GRETEL: Oh no!
WITCH: Stop that wailing or I will cook you first! Now we must use this big stove. Go at once to the yard and bring logs for the fire.
GRETEL: But....
WITCH: No buts! Go I say! *(she advances threateningly on Gretel, cackling)*

GRETEL runs off. EXITS

The Witch goes into a bizarre wild dance around the stage, chanting as she twirls

WITCH: Hubble, bubble, cauldron bubble,
                   It's time to stew the brat.
                   I'll mix herbs and spices and add a little fat.
                   Then boil and simmer, poach or fry,
                   Baste and roast or griddle.
                   So now to open up the stove and pop him in the middle!
                   Hee, tree, tree, tree.

The Witch pauses to think and then executes another cackling war dance

                   Why waste fuel on cooking one
                   When there's room enough for two.
                   Now I'm in a baking mood and really on my mettle,
                   I'll saute, pan fry, casserole that scrummy little Gretel.
                   Sugar and spice and all things nice,
                   We know all girls are good,
                   So I'll sugar coat and frost her and have her as my pud!

GRETEL ENTERS with logs and a smudged, tearful face

WITCH: Ah, there you are.

She moves to the stove and flings open the oven door. Dull flickering light is seen inside. Gretel cries in alarm and drops the logs. Hansel, frightened, grips his bars

GRETEL: Oh please, please don't do this. I will work for you, be your servant, cook, clean....
WITCH: Silence! The oven must be really hot. Throw in the logs!

Gretel throws logs through the door. Shafts of bright flickering red lights show

WITCH: Ah! See how it burns! Tell me when the oven is hot enough.
GRETEL: How can I tell?
WITCH: Stupid girl! Look inside of course.
GRETEL: I am looking.
WITCH: No, put your head right in.
GRETEL: I don't understand.
WITCH: What a ridiculous child. Stand aside, I'll show you.

Witch goes to the oven, puts her head in and then her shoulders. Gretel runs behind her giving her a mighty push. The Witch, shouting, is half way into the oven. Gretel reaches into Witch's pocket, pulling out the key which she shows to audience

GRETEL: The key! I have the key to the cage!

Witch is kicking her legs and crying out. Gretel runs to the cage and unlocks it. Hansel jumps out and both run to behind Witch, pushing and pushing until she is all inside. They slam the door and stand back, triumphant. Two jets of smoke issue from the stove. The Witch's cries fade to stop

Lighting changes can be used during this sequence, then up to full

HANSEL: Wow! We've done it. We have destroyed the wicked Witch!
GRETEL: Won't everyone be pleased!
HANSEL: Yes, if we ever see home again.
GRETEL: Someone will rescue us.
HANSEL: But don't forget that this gingerbread house is magic to trap hungry people like we were.
GRETEL: What shall we do?
HANSEL: I don't know.
GRETEL: Hansel, this must be the Witch who stole the Prince's money.
HANSEL: Yes, I wonder if it is hidden here? Let's look.

They search about the room, Hansel going behind the cage, where he calls

HANSEL: Gretel! Here!
GRETEL: What is it? *(she goes to side of cage)*
HANSEL: There's a trap door back here and it's not locked
GRETEL: Open it at once.
HANSEL: I'm reaching in and... hey, what's this? *(he brings out a handful of jewelry, handing it to Gretel)* There's more... and sacks. Of coins I think. *(he hands out two small sacks)*

Gretel looks into one

GRETEL: It must be the Prince's treasure!
HANSEL: Hooray!

They dance around the room. Gretel puts the jewelry into the open sack

GRETEL: Hansel, how are we ever going to get this home?
HANSEL: Well it will be dark again before we can get through the forest. Let's sleep and first thing tomorrow we must try to find our way.

They take a sack of coins each, and using them as pillows, lay down on the floor

TABS CLOSE on the scene

Apron scene follows while next scene is set

A CHILD as a MOUSE peeps on, ENTERS, turns and beckons. SEVERAL MORE MICE ENTER and gather around her

MOUSE: Guess what I've heard!
OTHERS: *(squeakily ad libbing chatter)* What? What have you heard]
MOUSE: Remember my cousin?
ANOTHER: What, the one that plays the mouth organ?
MOUSE: Yes, our Monica.
ANOTHER: What about her?
MOUSE: She lives in Witch Hazel's house.
ANOTHER: The one that's made of gingerbread and sweets?
MOUSE: Yes.
ANOTHER: That's very brave. And very silly.
MOUSE: Well she is a sugar mouse. And she told me that the wicked witch is dead.
OTHERS: No!
MOUSE: Yes. She has been burnt.
ANOTHER: At the stake?
MOUSE: No, she was about to make a steak with two children but they cooked her instead.
OTHERS: Hooray! That means we can live in peace. Hooray!

MUSIC CUE 19

MOUSE DANCE. This can be a movement to music of playing games. Hopscotch, skipping, ring o' roses etc. ending in all fall down and much laughter. On applause they take a bow

MOUSE: I've had a brilliant idea. Now there is no longer anyone in the gingerbread house we can eat it!
ANOTHER: But only hungry people can see it.
ALL: We are always hungry!

They crowd to the centre as

TABS OPEN ON SCENE THREE

SCENE THREE

THE DENSE FOREST. Lighting full. The outside of the gingerbread house is set. The MICE spread out and tiptoe toward it, at the last moment making a dash, squeaking, chatting noisily, gather around it and mime pulling pieces off and eating them. In their excitement they slowly push the piece of scenery off until the Gingerbread house and they have vanished into the wings. And there on the stage lay HANSEL and GRETEL asleep on the treasure

ZIPPY ENTERS slowly, tired. Is crossing upstage when he sees the sleepers. Stops, looks again, perks up happily and starts to move around the stage in an abandoned leggy dance, ending puffed out. His rear sits on the stage and the front part sits on the rear's lap. On applause he gets up and takes a bow

HANSEL and GRETEL awake toward the end of the dance and run to him as he bows

BOTH: Zippy! It's dear old Zippy!
HANSEL: Zippy, do you know the way home?

Zippy nods

GRETEL: Will you take us there?

Zippy nods

DAME ENTERS

DAME: Zippy, where have you got to,... ah there you are!
HANSEL and **GRETEL:** Hello, Dame Dotty!
DAME: Hansel! Gretel! *(she calls off)* Everybody! Come quick. The children are here!

Some of the GIPSY CHORUS ENTER, excited, ad libbing. WOODCUTTER and TOMMY ENTER

WOODCUTTER: Children!
BOTH: Father!

They run to him and embrace

WOODCUTTER: My darlings, are you alright? I've been so worried about you and so angry with myself.
HANSEL: Don't fret, father. We understand.
GRETEL: And we are quite alright.
DAME: What happened? Where have you been?
HANSEL: We were lured into Witch Hazel's cottage.

All react as REST OF CHORUS ENTER

TOMMY: The wicked Witch?
WOODCUTTER: Where is her cottage? I will kill her!
GRETEL: Her cottage was right here, but it has gone, the forest mice have eaten it.
HANSEL: And the Witch is dead.
ALL: *(ad. lib)* Dead?
WOODCUTTER: How did that happen?
HANSEL: We melted her in the stove.
ALL: *(ad lib)* The Witch is dead. Hooray! The wicked Witch is dead!

MUSIC CUE 20

SONG & ROUTINE. (See music suggestions) DAME, TOMMY, WOODCUTTER, HANSEL, GRETEL, ZIPPY, CHORUS. On applause a FANFARE SOUNDS

CHORUS: Here comes the Prince!

DANCERS as HUNTSMEN ENTER, forming a line as a guard of honour. PRINCE ENTERS arm in arm with ROSE. Cast bow or curtsy

ALL: Your Highness!
DAME: Our Rose!

Dame has curtsied but now falls to floor with surprise

DAME: What are you doing with Mr Prince?

Tommy helps her up

ROSE: We were looking for the lost children, but we found one another.
PRINCE: And your daughter has consented to walk out with me.
DAME: Och, what can I say? I'm so flustered. I'm all of a twist.
TOMMY: Oliver Twist? What's he got to do with it?
DAME: Well, he got in a dickens of a state. Just fancy, my daughter going out with a Prince!
PRINCE: And I am very happy about that, but even happier to hear the wonderful news about the Witch.
TOMMY: Yes, Hansel and Gretel did it.
ALL: Hooray!
PRINCE: I must find a way of rewarding you.
HANSEL: Perhaps sir, the return of your treasure will help.
PRINCE: My treasure?
GRETEL: Yes sir. I think we have found it.

She goes to the two sacks and carries them to the Prince, who looks inside one

PRINCE: It is indeed my treasure!

HANSEL: We found it in the Witch's cottage.

PRINCE: Well done indeed! Now there really must be celebrations. Tomorrow I will hold a grand party at my palace, and everyone is invited.

ALL: Hooray!

WOODCUTTER: And I really must get my children home.

DAME: Zippy can do the honours.

Zippy comes forward. Gretel is lifted onto his back and he leads a parade around the stage, Woodcutter leading him. Hansel is held shoulder high and chaired by two chorus men. Prince and Rose follow and then Dancers and chorus

MUSIC CUE 21

GRAND PARADE. All are EXITING except DAME & TOMMY who remain on Apron as...

TABS CLOSE on the scene

TOMMY: Things have worked out just great, haven't they ma.

DAME: Super. It makes me want to sing.

TOMMY: Oh no!

DAME: Yes, but only something with easy words.

TOMMY: What about Supercalifragilisticexpialidocious?

DAME: Yes that sounds easy.

TOMMY: I'll help you. Are you ready? After three... three!

MUSIC CUE 22

DUET & SONG SHEET. DAME and TOMMY. Any song here but Supercali... is suggested. They sing one chorus

TOMMY: I bet the audience can't sing that one.

DAME: Of course they can.

TOMMY: Never.

DAME: Let's ask them. Can you sing that one with us?

AUDIENCE: Yes.

DAME: Both of you, eh? I said, can you sing that song?

AUDIENCE: Yes!

DAME: Smashing. All together then, one, two, three.

She conducts and they sing along one chorus

TOMMY: Very good, but I think a few were having a little trouble. Getting their califragi mixed up with their fragilistic.

DAME: They need the words.

TOMMY: There's no chance of getting them, here in the forest.

DAME: We need someone to try and find them. Would any two children like to help us?

They select two children from audience and bring them on stage, asking names and where from etc.

DAME: You look like two clever children. Do you think you could magic the words for us?

TOMMY: Course you can.

DAME: I bet they can't.

TOMMY: Oh yes they can.

DAME: Oh no they can't.

TOMMY: They will be able to if I sprinkle them with a little magic oofle dust.

He takes a little glitter from his pocket and sprinkles it over them

DAME: That's it, off you go. This way.

She guides them off into the wings where the stage manager puts them either side of a board with the words on

DAME: While our friends are looking for the words, let's get a few more of you up on stage.

Dame and Tommy go into audience and select children. Ideally, SEVEN. They can all be interviewed if required

DAME: Right, now we are ready to sing.

On this cue the stage manager sends the two children on with the songsheet board which they hold throughout the song

TOMMY: How clever, they have found the words!

Words on board as follows:

> SUPER CALI FRAGI LISTIC EXPI ALI DOCIOUS
> EVEN THOUGH THE SOUND OF IT IS SOMETHING QUITE ATROCIOUS,
> IF YOU SAY IT LOUD ENOUGH YOU'LL ALWAYS SOUND PRECOCIOUS,
> SUPER CALI FRAGI LISTIC EXPI ALI DOCIOUS.

Dame and Tommy then get each child to sing one section of song title each, going along the line, then all together for rest of song. The song can be repeated in unison with audience if more time wanted for set change. On applause Dame tells children how good they were and each is rewarded with a wrapped sweet as they return to seats. Tommy takes over the song board

DAME: Come on our Tommy we must get into our party clothes and get along to the Palace.

DAME and TOMMY EXIT calling cheerio to audience. Tommy takes the songboard off

TABS OPEN ON SCENE FOUR

SCENE FOUR

BALLROOM OF THE PALACE. Full Set. Lighting full

MUSIC CUE 23

DANCE. DANCERS and CHORUS. Company are dressed for a party. Dancers can do a speciality section. A FLUNKEY stands at entrance.

FLUNKEY: Please welcome the Prince and Miss Rose.

PRINCE and ROSE ENTER. Company applaud and bow

PRINCE: My friends, I hope you are all enjoying the party. So on with the dance.

Reprise of dance number with Prince and Rose leading. End of number...

PRINCE: My friends, I have a special announcement to make. I am happy to tell you that Rose and I are now engaged.
ALFREDO: Three cheers for the happy couple.
ALL: Hooray, hooray, hooray!

MUSIC CUE 24

DUET. PRINCE, ROSE and COMPANY. Company join on second chorus. On applause....

FLUNKEY: Please welcome our heroes, Hansel and Gretel with their father.

HANSEL, GRETEL and WOODCUTTER ENTER. Chorus applaud and cheer

PRINCE: Hello children. We are all so proud of you.
HANSEL and **GRETEL:** Thank you sir.
PRINCE: *(to Woodcutter)* My dear sir, you are most welcome. But where is your wife?
WOODCUTTER: My wife, the children's step mother, has decided to leave. She could not face what she had done and so has left me. And I must say that I am not sorry.
ALL: Hooray!
PRINCE: And now I must reward you.
WOODCUTTER: It is Hansel and Gretel who should be rewarded.
PRINCE: Well, I have a special gift for them. A playhouse that has two delightful rooms. One is full of sweets that can be eaten without fear of a Witch, and the other is filled with toys which I know they have never enjoyed.
HANSEL and **GRETEL:** How wonderful. Thank you sir.

ROSE: And here are some of the toys now!

MUSIC CUE 25

TOY PARADE. CHILDREN. CHILDREN ENTER in a parade or dance either dressed as toys (Soldier, Clown, Ballerina, Teddy Bear etc) or carrying them. Solo dance as wind up doll etc can be performed. Number ends with children in two groups either side of stage. Cast are delighted and applaud

PRINCE: And you master woodcutter are welcome to my staff. There is a permanent position for you here at the palace, with a salary to keep you and your children in comfort for the rest of your days.
WOODCUTTER: *(bowing)* You are indeed generous sir. Thank you.
FLUNKEY: Please welcome Tommy..

TOMMY ENTERS

TOMMY: Hi kids!
AUDIENCE: Hi Tommy!
TOMMY: Hi Prince!
PRINCE: Low Tommy.
TOMMY: Ooh, you made a funny again.
PRINCE: Well we haven't had a joke for a while.
TOMMY: And it wasn't much of one then. I'll tell you some good jokes when I get around to it.
ROSE: You know I really love Tommy. He is my idol. I don't know anyone more idle.
PRINCE: I hear you have ambition to be a champion sausage maker.
TOMMY: Yes I'll string along with that.
PRINCE: Then why don't you go into training with the S.A.S?
TOMMY: The S.A.S.?
PRINCE: The Sausage Appreciation Society.
TOMMY: What a good idea. I will when I get around to it.
PRINCE: Flunkey, please come forward.

The Flunkey marches to the Prince with a box. Then returns to position. Prince opens it and takes out a large gold coloured disc with the words A ROUND TUIT. boldly printed on it

Please accept with my compliments this Round Tuit.
TOMMY: Wow! Thank you very much!
ROSE: There we are, our Tommy, you will always be able to get around to things now.
FLUNKEY: Ladies and gentlemen, it is cabaret time! Tonight the Prince has brought to you... at enormous expense... the one and only... Dame Dotty!

DAME ENTERS with a pair of roller skates strung around her neck

DAME: Coo... ee! It's me the grand diva.
TOMMY: Diver? Are they your diver's boots?

DAME: I said Diva, not Diver. I want to sing in opera. I've always fancied myself in the role of Carmen. And these are my Carmen Rollers.

ROSE: I didn't know you could sing opera, ma.

DAME: Oh yes, I used to do duets with 'our ada'.

PRINCE: So you want to sing in opera?

DAME: Yes please.

MUSIC CUE 26

COMIC SONG. DAME. Suggest "I Want To Sing In Opera" This must be sung comically with wrong notes, sometimes flat etc. But with plenty of power. She collapses into Prince's arm at the end. All applaud

PRINCE: I've heard of supporting the arts, but this is ridiculous!

DAME: Ooh, sorry your princeship. But I enjoyed that. *(she straightens up)*

ROSE: You certainly sing with feeling, ma.

TOMMY: And if she had any real feeling she wouldn't sing.

DAME: I'll have you know that I have a large repertoire.

TOMMY: And that dress makes it look worse.

DAME: When I sing, people clap their hands.

TOMMY: Yes, over their ears.

DAME: Can't you send me away to study singing, Mr Prince?

WOODCUTTER: Yes, send her as far as you can.

PRINCE: No I haven't enough notes, but because I am in a generous mood, I would like to appoint you governess to Hansel and Gretel, with your own apartment in the palace.

DAME: Oh I should love that. No more travelling. And looking after the woodcutter's two little chips off the old block.

Hansel and Gretel run to her

PRINCE: And as a bonus you can be the permanent teacher in the palace to all the village children.

CHILDREN; Hooray!

DAME: Oh no! What have I done to deserve that! Never mind kids, what I will do is make the lessons an hour shorter each day. So the lessons will lessen.

CHILDREN: Hooray for Dame Dotty!

PRINCE: Now who have I left out? Rose my dear, borrow my Access card and order your wedding dress. But don't leave me for long.

ROSE: I won't my love. Access makes the heart grow fonder.

PRINCE: So there we are, all are happy.

ALFREDO: Wait. What about Zippy? He found Hansel and Gretel.

ALL: *(ad lib)* Yes, what about Zippy?

PRINCE: Fetch him at once.

TOMMY: No need. Here he comes!

ZIPPY trots IN. All applaud and welcome him

DAME: My, you look nippy, Zippy!

PRINCE: You see, I hadn't forgotten. Flunkey!

Flunkey comes forward with a bright silk sash and a rosette which the Prince takes, placing them on Zippy. Zippy bends a knee and bows

I name Zippy chief stallion of my stable, who will occupy the royal horse box and carry my lovely Rose to our wedding.

ALL: Hooray!

MUSIC CUE 27

SONG & ROUTINE. FULL COMPANY. (See music suggestions) On applause the principals come into line facing audience. TOMMY. DAME. ROSE. PRINCE. HANSEL. GRETEL, WOODCUTTER

HANSEL: Seeing the Witch being finally boiled,

GRETEL: We hope that your fun was not much spoiled.

DAME: Rose has found the Prince of her dreams,

TOMMY: And the Prince can fulfil all his wealthy schemes.

ROSE: Tommy has finally got a round tuit,

PRINCE: But teaching the children, Dame Dotty may rue it.

WOODCUTTER: Hansel and Gretel are happy at last, with a cottage to play in and no need to fast.

ALL SEVEN: We hope you've had a happy time, and really enjoyed our pantomime...

WHOLE COMPANY: Goodnight!

REPRISE SONG 27

FULL COMPANY

CURTAIN

WALK DOWN. CALLS

FINAL CURTAIN

PRODUCTION NOTES

CASTING: Assuming a traditional male Dame and female Prince the casting is: PRINCIPALS, 3 male, 4 female, plus Boy and Girl for Hansel and Gretel, 2 male minor roles and 1 female minor role from chorus. 2 people for Zippy the horse. The chorus can be of any size, ideally not less than 6 with 6 Dancers and 8 children, 2 of whom have a little dialogue.

WOODCUTTER: Small acting role, middle aged man. A demure character under his wife's thumb, who becomes more authoritative later. No solos, but sings once with group and once with company.

WOODCUTTER'S WIFE: Small acting role. Middle aged. Strong character, but not as much a baddie as the Witch. No singing.

HANSEL: Boy should appear about 10 years of age, small and slight if possible. Good at dialogue and able to sing nicely. Sings 2 duets and in 4 group numbers.

GRETEL: Preferably slightly younger than Hansel, also small and slight. A nice little actress, able to sing sweetly and move well. Sings 2 duets and in 4 group numbers.

ALFREDO: Small character part. A sturdy leader, also member of chorus. No solo singing.

TOMMY: Very personable lively young man who must have rapport with young audiences, and good at comedy timing. Sings in 4 group numbers plus songsheet with Dame.

DAME DOTTY: The traditional Dame. Bizarre, comic, full of life but also warm hearted and sympathetic. Must have good comedy timing and strong rapport with audience. Ideally played by a middle aged or older male. Should be able to put over 1 Comic Song. Also sings in 4 group numbers plus Songsheet with Tommy.

ROSE: Principal Girl. Young, around 20. Nice 'girl next door', with some comedy lines. Should move well. Dances with Prince and should be a good singer. 1 solo. 2 duets and 4 group numbers.

PRINCE: Principal Boy. Usually played by female. Young but older and preferably taller than Rose. Leggy, of good bearing and nice speaking voice. Dances with Rose and should sing well, blending with Rose for 2 duets. Also sings in 3 group numbers.

WITCH HAZEL: A really strong character part. Slimy but nice to start and then a cackling hag. No singing.

FAIRY: Small speaking part, ideally the leading dancer.

ZIPPY: Two agile people with good sense of movement, mime and timing who can work together. No speaking or singing.

FLUNKEY: Chorus member with a few lines that must be delivered clearly with authority.

CHORUS: Appear throughout as gipsies, but in party clothes for the finale. Do some 'cross overs' and odd lines and reactions. Should all move well and sing/dance in 7 numbers.

DANCERS: Appear in 7 routines as Gipsies, Fairies, Elves, Huntsmen and Birds in Ballet and traditional/modern including singing with the chorus.

CHILDREN: As Gipsies, Mice, Birds, Fairies, Toys with odd lines and reactions particularly in the school and fairy story scenes. Must all dance and sing. Appear in 10 dance and/or singing numbers.

MUSIC AND DANCE

The amount of music and the titles listed are **suggestions only** Your M.D. and Choreographer may of course use any suitable music that 'carries' the story and must choose their own Ballet dance and background pieces. No panto song should be too long and preferably should be well known.

Please note that permission to perform this play **does not** include permission to use copyright songs and music suggested here. Where copyright exists elsewhere, or if in any doubt, performers are urged to consult **The Performing Right Society**.

Music suggested:

ACT ONE

CUE 1.	P. 1.	'This Is Our Once A Year Day' Song/Routine. or 'It's The Most Wonderful Day Of The Year' or 'When You're Smiling'. CHORUS, DANCERS, CHILDREN.
CUE 2.	P. 4.	'Someone To Watch Over Me'. Song. ROSE. or 'Someday My Prince Will Come'.
CUE 3.	P. 8.	'Always Look On The Bright Side Of Life'. Song/Routine or 'Put On A Happy Face'. HANSEL, GRETEL, DAME, ZIPPY, CHILDREN.
CUE 4.	P. 11.	'Where Is Love'. Duet. HANSEL, GRETEL.
CUE 5.	P. 11.	Choreographer's choice. Mice Dance. CHILDREN Possibly something from Nutcracker.
CUE 6.	P. 13.	Choreographer's choice. Ballet DANCERS.
CUE 7.	P. 14.	'Teddy Bears Picnic'. Song/routine. CHILDREN
CUE 8.	P. 17.	'I Was Born With A Smile On My Face'. Song/routine. DAME, TOMMY, ROSE, HANSEL, GRETEL, 5 CHILDREN
CUE 9.	P. 19.	'Song Of The Mounties'. Song and March. CHORUS. (From Rose Marie) or any hunting type march.
CUE 10.	P. 20.	'Post Horn Gallop' Dance. DANCERS.
CUE 11.	P. 21.	'When I Fall In Love'. Duet. PRINCE/ROSE. 'Or The Girl That I Marry'. or 'I Only Have Eyes For You'.
CUE 12.	P. 22.	Any silly song or nursery rhyme for ghost gag. Trio. TOMMY, ROSE, PRINCE.
CUE 13.	P. 24.	Choreographer's Choice. Bird Ballet. DANCERS, CHILDREN. (Perhaps Swan Lake)
CUE 14.	P. 24.	A mystical piece of off stage choral music. CHORUS. I suggest the opening passage from Brigadoon, 'Once in the Highlands' etc, Or, alternatively this could be music only, using perhaps 'Morning' from Peer Gynt.
CUE 15.	P. 25.	Only a few dramatic chords as Tabs close on Act 1.

ACT 2

CUE 16.	P. 26.	Bright Gipsy music required or any of the 3 titles suggested to open Act One.Song/Movement. CHORUS.
CUE 17.	P. 26.	Taped Pan Pipe or that recorded by James Galway such as 'Le Basque' (by Marin Marcus) for first section with 'Liebeafreud' (Kreisler) for second section. Dance. CHILDREN, DANCERS.
CUE 18.	P. 32.	'Wouldn't It Be Lovely'. Duet. HANSEL, GRETEL..
CUE 19.	P. 37.	'Girls And Boys Come Out To Play'. Routine. CHILDREN.
CUE 20.	P. 39.	'Ding Dong The Witch Is Dead'. (Wizard Of Oz) Song and Routine. DAME, TOMMY, WOODCUTTER, HANSEL, GRETEL, ZIPPY, CHORUS.
CUE 21.	P. 40.	'March Of The Siamese Children'. (King And I) Parade. MUSIC ONLY.
CUE 22.	P. 40.	'Supercalifragilistic'. Songsheet number. DAME, TOMMY. Or 'If You're Happy And You Know It Clap Your Hands'. Or any simple ditty.
CUE 23.	P. 42.	Any Waltz or Gavotte. Dance. DANCERS, CHORUS, PRINCE, ROSE.
CUE 24.	P. 42.	'The Perfect Year' (Sunset Boulevard) Duet. ROSE, PRINCE. (Has the line... 'We don't need a crowded ballroom')
CUE 25.	P. 43.	'Parade Of The Tin Soldiers'. Parade/Dance. CHILDREN. For a SOLO DANCE, 'The Doll Song' or 'Doll On A Music Box'. (Chitty Chitty Bang Bang)
CUE 26.	P. 44.	'I Want To Sing In Opera'. Comic song. DAME.
CUE 27.	P. 45.	Reprise opening chorus. Song/Routine. FULL COMPANY.

SETTINGS

3 FULL. 2 INSETS. TABS OR FRONTCLOTH.

ACT 1. Scene 1 and 4. ACT 2. Scene 1. A CLEARING IN THE FOREST. FULL SET. Backloth of trees and foliage, perhaps a little sky showing. Tree wings and borders. Woodcutter's Cottage preferably on a truck with a practical door and a backing. This can be turned around to make interior for later scene. Caravan front also on a truck with entrance and rostrum behind and steps to entrance.

ACT 1. Scene 2. INSIDE THE WOODCUTTER'S COTTAGE. INSET. The cottage truck turned around Or two book flats. to show interior.

ACT 1. Scene 3 and 5. Act 2. Scene 3. THE DENSE FOREST. FULL SET. The same basic set as the Forest Clearing with cottage and caravan struck and extra borders wings, and if possible a cut cloth added. NO BLUE SKY should be seen. The Gingerbread Cottage exterior that travels on during action should be free standing and on castors for pushing off later. Ideally with a practical door. The cottage should be colourful with painted sweets and gingerbreads. Polestyrene pieces stuck on to give depth. Bits of these can be pulled of for children and mice to mime eating.

ACT 2. Scene 2. INSIDE THE GINGERBREAD COTTAGE. LARGER INSET. A cloth with two side wings behind curtain runners for as much depth as possible, and space for the large cage and stove. Ideally the cage shoud be raised on a rostrum.

ACT 2. Scene 4. BALLROOM OF THE PALACE. FULL SET. Make as opulent as you can. A staircase and chandelier if possible and rich drapes.

THE APRON SUB SCENES CAN BE PLAYED AGAINST TABS OR CLOTH.

PROPS LIST

ACT ONE

Scene 1.   Shopping bag with wrapped sweets.
              Axe.
              Ball.

Scene 2.   Wooden table and chair.
              Mixing bowl and spoon.
              Stones. (At least six, covered with luminous paint or foil)

Scene 3.   Bread in a cloth. (2 large pieces)
              Blanket of leaves.

Scene 4.   Benches to seat 9
              Handbell.
              Register.
              2 Satchels.
              9 Picture Boards. (Described on page 16 of script)
              Small round loaf.
              Walking stick.
              Butterfly net.
              Fishing rod.
              Nets.
              Gun.
              Bow and arrow.
              Handcuffs.
              Catapult.

ACT TWO

Scene 1.   Garlands.
              Flowers.
              Fruit baskets.
              Golden goblets.
              Decorative pedestal and bowl. (As a fountain)
              Carrier bag with Coloured tennis ball, Table tennis ball and long Rubber
              Tube with Funnel one end.

Scene 2.   Table and 2 chairs.
              Large key.
              Food bowl.
              Chicken bone.
              Birch broom.
              Logs.
              Jewelry.
              2 small bulging sacks.

Scene 3.   Glitter dust.
            Songsheet.
            Wrapped sweets.

Scene 4.   Toys for toy parade if children do not themselves represent toys.
            Box with large gold disc having bold words: A ROUND TUIT.
            Roller skates.
            Bright sash and rosette.

COSTUME CHANGES

WOODCUTTER: Workman's trousers and shirt. Neckerchief. Dull colours. Changes for final scene into colourful trousers, shirt and waistcoat.

WOODCUTTER'S WIFE: Long black dress with apron. No changes.

HANSEL: Short trousers. Shirt. Plain tunic. Changes for final scene with fancy waistcoat.

GRETEL: Plain dress. Change for final scene into pretty dress, bows in hair etc.

ALFREDO: Gipsy as chorus. Change for final scene.

TOMMY: Workaday Breeches and hose. Bright check shirt, neckerchief. Boots. Change for final scene with brighter colours, fancy waistcoat.

DAME DOTTY: Act 1. S. 1. Polka dot dress. Large multi coloured dots. Clashing coloured wig. Striped stockings. Huge Ear Rings etc. Act 1. S. 4. Teacher's Cap and gown over costume. Later, walking things..Bobble hat, walking boots. Act 1. S. 5. Still in walking things. Act 2. S. 1. Complete change. A different bizarre dress and accessories. Different wig. Act 2. S. 5. Further complete change for party. Different wig.

ROSE: Simple but pretty dress. Better one for final scene

PRINCE: Tunic, frilled shirt, tights, high boots, tricorn hat all colourful. Complete change for final scene.

WITCH HAZEL: All black long dress perhaps with green streaks. Wispy trailing sleeves. Black buttoned pointed shoes. Black hat.

FAIRY: Traditional with wand.

ZIPPY: Horse costume. Black shoes.

FLUNKEY: Tunic, hose, buckled shoes, powdered wig.

CHORUS: Gipsy skirts and blouses or trousers and shirts. All colourful. All change to smarter party clothes for final scene.

DANCERS. Act 1. S. 1 and S. 2 Gipsies. Act 1. S. 3 and 4 Mixture of Sprites, Fairies and Elves. Act 1. S. 5 Huntsmen, then Birds. Act 2. S. 1 and 2 Fairies. Act 2. S. 3 Huntsmen. Act 2. S. 4 Party clothes or adaptions of gipsy costumes.

CHILDREN. Act 1. S. 1 Gipsies. Act 1. S. 2 and 3 Mice. Act 1. S. 4 Gipsies. Act 1. S. 5 Birds. Act 2. S. 1 Fairies. Act 2. S. 2 and 3 Mice. Act 2 S. 4 Toys. See script P. 60.

LIGHTING AND EFFECTS

ACT 1. Scene 1.   Sunny day. Full.
                               P. 2. Smoke from Zippy's nostrils.
        Scene 2.   Cottage interior dimly lit.
                               P.11. Brighter lights for dance. Follow spot if possible.
                               End of dance check back to dim room.
        Scene 3.   Use darker colours, with green for deeper forest effect.
                               P. 13. Slow fade into night during ballet. A U/V sequence can be used during ballet. Moonlight to filter through trees and spotlight Hansel and Gretel.
        Scene 4.   Sunny day. Full.
        Scene 5.   As Scene 3.
                               P. 20. Sound Post Horn or Trumpet.
P. 22 Dim for ghost scene with green follow spot on each entry of Witch.
P. 24. Slow fade as Hansel & Gretel go to sleep, then change of colours for bird ballet, with follow spot on last bird to exit. Then colours change to moonlight.
P. 24. Smoke machine to cover cottage setting, or fade to blackout. Then dawn breaks, warm colours cross fade with moonlight.
P. 25. Highlight Witch's cottage when Hansel and Gretel see it.

ACT 2. Scene 1.   Sunny day. Full.
        Scene 2.   Interior. Full.
P. 32. Check to blackout. Pause, then slow to full.
P. 33. Repeat.
P. 35. Flickering fire glow when stove door opens. Brighter when logs thrown into stove.
P. 36. Jets of smoke from stove. General flashing lights can be used during struggle with Witch into stove. P.50.
        Scene 3.   As previous dense forest.
P. 39. Trumpet fanfare.
        Scene 4.   Interior. Rich colours. Chandelier if possible.

All apron scenes, general illumination. No cues.